Mary Ann Bell, EdD
Bobby Ezell, EdD
James L. Van Roekel, MLS

Cybersins and Digital Good Deeds
A Book About Technology and Ethics

Pre-publication
REVIEWS,
COMMENTARIES,
EVALUATIONS . . .

"*Cybersins and Digital Good Deeds* presents an amazingly broad collection of short essays that address how technology impacts our lives and requires new considerations of old questions: 'What is right?' and 'What is wrong?' Written in a manner that will well-serve today's multitaskers, each essay can be read in a short period of time. My recommendation for readers is to treat each chapter in this book as the source for a brief daily period of reflection on ethical decision-making in the Information Age."

Nancy E. Willard, MS, JD
Director, Center for Safe
and Responsible Internet Use

"This book explains in layperson's terms the familiar and unfamiliar language of technology use, and offers insight into the positive and/or negative impact of that use. Technology opens up such a vast global arena for communication, entertainment, shopping, learning, the same activities we have always done, but with the potential to impact so many more people than ever before. *Cybersins and Digital Good Deeds* alerts readers to the value or threat of technology use and misuse that can affect us all."

Jan Robin, MEd, BS
Instructional Technology Specialist,
Conroe Independent School District

The Haworth Press®
New York • London • Oxford

Cybersins and Digital Good Deeds

A Book About Technology and Ethics

THE HAWORTH PRESS
Titles of Related Interest

Cybersins and Digital Good Deeds
A Book About Technology and Ethics

Mary Ann Bell, EdD
Bobby Ezell, EdD
James L. Van Roekel, MLS

The Haworth Press®
New York • London • Oxford

For more information on this book or to order, visit
http://www.haworthpress.com/store/product.asp?sku=5632

or call 1-800-HAWORTH (800-429-6784) in the United States and Canada
or (607) 722-5857 outside the United States and Canada

or contact orders@HaworthPress.com

Published by

The Haworth Press, Inc., 10 Alice Street, Binghamton, NY 13904–1580.

PUBLISHER'S NOTE
The development, preparation, and publication of this work has been undertaken with great care. However, the Publisher, employees, editors, and agents of The Haworth Press are not responsible for any errors contained herein or for consequences that may ensue from use of materials or information contained in this work. The Haworth Press is committed to the dissemination of ideas and information according to the highest standards of intellectual freedom and the free exchange of ideas. Statements made and opinions expressed in this publication do not necessarily reflect the views of the Publisher, Directors, management, or staff of The Haworth Press, Inc., or an endorsement by them.

Cover design by Karen Lowe.

Library of Congress Cataloging-in-Publication Data

Bell, Mary Ann.
    Cybersins and digital good deeds : a book about technology and ethics / Mary Ann Bell, Bobby Ezell, James L. Van Roekel.
       p. cm.
    Includes bibliographical references and index.
    ISBN-13: 978-0-7890-2953-9 (case : alk. paper)
    ISBN-10: 0-7890-2953-7 (case : alk. paper)
    ISBN-13: 978-0-7890-2954-6 (soft : alk. paper)
    ISBN-10: 0-7890-2954-5 (soft : alk. paper)
    1. Computers—Moral and ethical aspects. 2. Internet—Moral and ethical aspects. 3. Computers—Social aspects. 4. Internet—Social aspects. 5. Technology—Moral and ethical aspects. I. Ezell, Bobby. II. Van Roekel, James L. III. Title.

QA76.9. B45 2006
303.48'34—dc22

                                  2006027200

CONTENTS

ABOUT THE AUTHORS

Mary Ann Bell, EdD, MLS, BA, is Assistant Professor in the Department of Library Science at Sam Houston State University in Texas, where she teaches classes related to technology and librarianship. She is co-author of *Internet and Personal Computing Fads* (Haworth). She has published articles and presented at numerous conferences on the topics of information ethics and creative teaching that incorporates technology. Dr. Bell is active in the Texas Library Association, American Library Association, Texas Computer Education Association, and Delta Kappa Gamma. In 2005 she was named Outstanding Researcher for the Sam Houston State University Department of Education.

Bobby Ezell, MEd, EdD, is an assistant professor for instructional technology in the College of Education at Sam Houston State University in Huntsville, Texas. Dr. Ezell has held a number of positions in education in grades K-12 including serving as an English teacher, a high school English department chair, a guidance counselor, an assistant principal for both student affairs and for curriculum, a high school principal, and an instructional technology coordinator. Also, he has held a number of positions in a private school, including service as an English teacher, technology director, and interim school head. In addition, Dr. Ezell taught English for many years in the North Harris Montgomery County Community College system. In 1991 he was one of ten teachers in the state named as an Outstanding Secondary Teacher in Texas, an award given annually by the University of Texas.

James L. Van Roekel, MLS, MA, is Director of Academic Instructional Technology and Distance Learning at Sam Houston State University in Texas. He is co-author of *Internet and Personal Computing Fads*. His research, publications, and teaching focus is on the investigation of the utilization of free and off-the-shelf hardware and software toward the development of multimedia and digital library applications in distance learning and Web-based broadcasting. He has been awarded two technology grants totaling more than $650,000 toward educating university faculty in thinking about and using technology and technology applications as well as creating multimedia subjects to foster international exchanges with former Communist countries in Eastern Europe.

Introduction

Technology has been heralded throughout history as a means for making people's lives better, and at the same time cursed as a dangerous threat to humanity. Both positions have examples to back up their claims. Technology has certainly led to inventions that save time, improve communication, make travel easier, decrease burdensome workloads, and even save lives. At the same time technology can threaten our privacy, our jobs, and even our personal safety. Essentially, technology is neutral, and the means by which new devices and methods are used determine its value or threat. The purpose of this book is to present recent trends, developments, devices, and ideas that may impact our lives positively and negatively.

This book is organized in much the same arrangement as many Haworth books, such as those in the fads encyclopedia series. While the topics included are not necessarily fads, the glossary format is useful for presentation. One intent behind the book is to demystify some of the terms often heard in threatening tones but perhaps not understood by the layperson. At the same time the content emphasizes that technology also offers many new and promising ways of improving lives. This book could be useful in high school and academic libraries, public libraries, and for general use by people wanting to become more informed about good and bad behavior involving technology. It offers particular interest to teachers, students, and other readers interested in clarifying issues related to information ethics.

Writers such as Neil Postman and Clifford Stoll have sought to discourage a headlong rush into the adoption of every new gizmo and program that comes along without first examining the costs, both financial and effectual. According to Postman, every decision one makes to acquire, learn, and implement a new technology also involves a converse decision not to do something else with one's time, energy, and money. Stoll warns that overenthusiastic technophiles are actually a danger to society. Further, there are numerous evident and

Cybersins and Digital Good Deeds
© 2007 by The Haworth Press, Inc. All rights reserved.
doi:10.1300/5632_a

worrisome situations where computer technology is used for unethical and illegal actions. On the other hand, many people who are enthusiastic about the promises of technology point out the improvements it offers to individual lives and to society as a whole.

This book offers a guide to the uninitiated regarding unfamiliar or little understood issues and terms regarding information ethics. Criteria for selection included historical importance, present relevance, and the likelihood of future impact. Issues discussed were selected to represent a variety of fields of interest, including general use, business, entertainment, multimedia development, and education. Readers with an interest in the effects of technology on today's society, both favorable and unfavorable, will find this book an interesting and informative choice.

Absent Presence

The way people communicate is evolving at a dizzying rate as we depend more and more upon electronic devices and less upon face-to-face interactions. Many people can be seen walking or sitting together in public places, with one or both talking on cell phones rather than conversing with each other. "Absent presence" is a psychological term used to describe the presence of someone whose attention is directed elsewhere. This experience is frustrating and upsetting to the

Why don't people sitting together talk to each other instead of distant parties via phones? (*Source*: © iStockphoto.com/Bryukhanova, Anna, "Young Couple Speaking Cell phones." Available at http//:www.istockphoto.com.)

Cybersins and Digital Good Deeds
© 2007 by The Haworth Press, Inc. All rights reserved.
doi:10.1300/5632_01

person who is left out. In fact the phenomenon is reaching the point that some people think it is making a permanent mark on modern culture and how people communicate and relate to one another. As the Internet and the use of cellular phones gain popularity as means of communication, there seems to be an attendant decrease in activities in which people engage with one another face to face. Proponents of electronic communication like to point out, quite rightly, that often such means result in closer ties over distances. For example, in times of national disaster, the Internet and cell phones have been instrumental in helping people reach out to one another. At the same time, however, our devices may separate us from others in our immediate presence.

BIBLIOGRAPHY

Berman, D. (2003). Technology Hodgepodge Adds to Life's Distractions. *The Wall Street Journal* (November 16), p. A7.

Advertising at School

Advertising is a part of the environment almost everywhere people go today. Ads are on billboards, sides of buses, benches in parks, and even the backs of restroom stalls. We hear and see them and accept this as part of the world in which we live. This has been true for many years. At one time, though, school students were relatively free of the distraction of commercial advertising, or at least were not constantly exposed to it. There was a time when ads were limited to minor intrusions such as the book covers provided by local businesses. Far from that are today's schools. Even the book covers have gone big business and are splashy colorful mini-billboards for any number of nationally known brands.

One big breakthrough in school advertising was the advent of Channel One in the 1990s. Schools yearning for adequate video equipment agreed to show the daily news broadcasts offered by this company in return for receiving classroom monitors. Cooperating schools had to promise to show the newscasts to all students daily, and not edit them in any way. The "catch" was that broadcasts were complete with commercials. There was some parental resistance, but for the most part the program was successful, and the door was opened for advertisers to enter the school environment. Some enterprising school administrators whose buildings are in airport landing paths have sold school roof space to advertisers so that passengers see ads as they land. One school district has even considered auctioning school names to corporations, so that citizens might be greeted by Pepsi Middle School or Coke High. The brand of soft drink and snack machines in a school is no longer coincidental. Companies such as Coca-Cola pay administrators for exclusive rights and prominent placement of their machines. Although big soft-drink distributors such as Coca-Cola, Pepsi, and Cadbury Schweppes say they are willingly pulling their high-sugar sodas from school machines, the companies continue to maintain powerful presences, offering bottled water and juice products instead. "Free" instructional materials may also be part of a curriculum, and carry along their own agendas. It is unlikely that nutritional materials supplied by Burger King will preach too stringently against our fast food culture.

The Internet has joined in the fray to win the attention of students with gusto. Corporations offer free equipment in return for banner ads or logos that appear on all screens. In some dot-com partnerships, companies may also gain personal information about student users in order to target them with ads that match their interests. One very well-known corporation, ZapMe!, gives schools computer labs that carry banner ads at all times while students use the equipment. The ads change frequently, thus exposing students to as many as 200 products during a class period. Also, students may be asked to respond to queries such as "survey question of the day." If a question was about favorite after-school activities, for example, then responses could be used to tailor future advertising. Advertisers have long recognized that school, the place where a highly coveted market audience spends most of its time, is an area that they want to penetrate. With technology, the options for doing so have mushroomed.

Why is this happening? Several reasons were cited in a recent Consumers Union survey. First, many schools are underfunded, a trend that shows no sign of reversal. Second, commercialism is increasingly prevalent in our culture in all other environments, with less and less resistance. Finally, children are a highly marketable group, apparently irresistible to advertisers (Labi, 1999).

Not all school and commercial partnerships should be viewed negatively. Some offer excellent opportunities for both the schools and the sponsors. Companies such as AT&T with its Learning Network and MCI with MarcoPolo have provided instructional content that is based on educational standards and offers students excellent learning resources. Companies that give refurbished computers to schools provide students with additional equipment and reduce waste that would result from simply discarding them. Many school districts work to provide each campus with a local corporate partner that works with that school to meet specific needs. Since schools are currently struggling with increasingly frustrating funding shortfalls, many joint business and school initiatives are mutually beneficial.

Indeed, what is the problem with a bit of commercialism in schools? One issue is that children are a captive audience. If parents do not want to expose children to commercials at home, it is easy to mute the ads or turn them off. If a child is sitting in a classroom, he or she cannot do the same. Young children especially lack the judgment to evaluate what they see and hear and separate hype from truth.

Clever marketers know this, and work to make their ads take advantage of this fact. Further, the mixing of advertising and instruction is troubling. If a student is researching a topic using online resources and at the same time being bombarded with banner advertisements, it is hard to know what he or she is assimilating. Further, some experts express concern about what effect such displays have on students' attention spans. Often this type of exposure occurs without parents' knowledge, and they might not be comfortable with the fact that information is being gathered about their children's interests and buying habits. Dot-com companies are already reaching children at home through television, radio, and Internet advertising. Marketing intrusions at school may help mold children into viewing relinquishment of personal privacy as something that is acceptable as they grow into adulthood, possibly making them more vulnerable as adults to commercial hypes and even scams.

What can be done to keep invasive and manipulative advertising out of schools? First, administrators need to be careful and selective of the offers they consider. They must wade through the legalese of agreements and weigh the benefits against the detriments of commercial ventures that involve students. There are no laws that specifically regulate corporate advertising in schools, though there are some efforts to address the issue. The National Association of State Boards of Education has set forth principles that school districts should follow to limit commercialism in schools. Educational researchers must follow guidelines for the use of human subjects in schools, and dot-com concerns should have the same restrictions for collection of student information. Educators should also be aware of the restrictions expressed in COPPA, the Children's Online Privacy Protection Act of 1998, which restricts online collection of personal information for children under the age of thirteen. Also, personal information from students must be only gathered in compliance with the Family Educational Rights and Privacy Act, which clearly states that parents must be informed of any third-party collection of such data. Some of the entities seeking entry into schools are directly in conflict with the aforementioned guidelines. School officials and parents must evaluate any and all commercial initiatives that involve advertising to students or gathering information from children, with the welfare of such students to be the prime consideration.

BIBLIOGRAPHY

Labi, N. (1999). Classrooms For Sale. *Time* 15 (April 19), pp. 44-46.

Soft Drink Companies Pull Products from Schools. (2006). *Beverage Industry* 97 (May), p. 6.

Willard, N. (2004). Capturing the "Eyeballs" and "E-wallets" of Captive Kids in School: Dot.com Invades Dot.edu. Available at http://www.csriu.org/online docs/documents/eyeballs.html. Accessed July 16, 2006.

AMBER Alert

The America's Missing: Broadcast Emergency Response (AMBER) Alert System began in 1996 when Dallas-Fort Worth police partnered with local broadcasters to develop an early warning system to help find abducted children. The system was created as a legacy to nine-year-old Amber Hagerman who was kidnapped while riding her bicycle in Arlington, Texas, and brutally murdered. When law enforcement has determined that a child abduction has occurred, and the abduction meets AMBER Alert criteria, broadcasters are notified and an alert is disseminated. AMBER Alerts are also issued on lottery tickets, wireless devices, and the Internet. Almost all of the fifty states are fully participating in the system, and many states broadcast alerts on special Web sites.

BIBLIOGRAPHY

U.S. Department of Justice. Frequently Asked Questions on AMBER Alert. Available at http://www.amberalert.gov/faqs.html. Accessed September 21, 2005.

Americans with Disabilities Act (ADA) and Its Impact upon Technology in Schools

The Americans with Disabilities Act (ADA), a federal civil rights act passed in 1990 to prohibit discrimination on the basis of a disability, provides those with physical handicaps access to the workplace and to government services. Because of the ADA public buildings are required to meet accessibility guidelines, and phone companies are required to provide accommodations for those with hearing or speech handicaps. The enforcement of ADA is charged to the Equal Employment Opportunity Commission.

In addition to its impact upon the rights of those with disabilities to compete for jobs and to have access to government and commercial services, the act has profoundly impacted the technology found in schools in two ways. First, the impact of the ADA is evident in the types of assistive technology used by students with physical, hearing, or visual handicaps. Highly specialized and personalized assistive technology gives students with physical handicaps the opportunity to function successfully in a learning environment. The operation of the technology may require the assistance of a teacher or instructional assistant. To assist with the purchase of such equipment and the training of personnel to operate it, the Assistive Technology Act became law in 1998 providing federal funding for the purchase of equipment and personnel training. The second impact of the ADA involves the development of capabilities placed into Windows operating systems to assist student users with hearing, speech, or physical handicaps.

The need to help handicapped youngsters function in educational settings has prompted the creation of highly specialized training programs for those who wish to assist students in using their support technology. The professional career position of assistive technology specialist has evolved. Programs for assistive technology specialists train personnel to act as a liaison with the regular classroom teachers by both addressing instructional needs of the handicapped youngster as well as assisting with assistive technology hardware or software used by the student.

Because of the ADA, public buildings are required to meet accessibility guide-lines, and phone companies are required to provide accommodations for those with hearing or speech handicaps. (*Source*: © iStockphoto.com/Ben Zirkel Stu-dio, "Man Wheelchair." Available at http://www.istockphoto.com.)

For youngsters and adults who may not need specialized assistive technology but experience certain speech, hearing, or accessibility limitations, computer operating systems provide options that may help. Handicap options in Windows XP, for example, include the following.

Accessibility Options to the Keyboard in Windows XP
- StickyKeys—Allows users to use commands one key at a time; for example, Shift, CTRL, ALT
- MouseKeys—Allows users to control the pointer with the numeric keyboard

- On-Screen Keyboards—Allows users to see a keyboard on-screen and to enter commands via the mouse
- Speech Recognition—Allows users to speak computer commands as well as to enter simple dictation using Word

Hearing Impaired Options in Windows XP
  - SoundSentry—Generates visual warning when a sound is made
  - Show Sounds—Tells program to display captions for speech and sound made within a program

Visually Impaired Options in Windows XP
  - Magnifier—Magnifies the area pointed to by the cursor in a space at the top of the screen; magnification size can be set to display up to nine times the normal screen size
  - ToggleKeys—Allows user to hear tones when pressing Caps Lock, Num Lock, and Scroll Lock

The Macintosh operating system offers many of the same options for users with hearing, speech, and physical handicaps. One particularly useful Macintosh capability is the built-in option of text to speech, a capability that allows the computer to read text to a user.

Video equipment also provides options that may assist the hearing impaired with closed caption capability.

BIBLIOGRAPHY

Lahm, E. A. (2003) Assistive Technology Specialists: Bringing Knowledge of Assistive Technology to School Districts. *Remedial and Special Education* 24(3), pp. 141-153.

Nelson, J. A. (Ed.). (1994). *The Disabled, the Media, and the Information Age.* Westport, CT: Greenwood Press.

White, E. A., Wepner, S. B., and Wetzel, D. C. (2003). Accessible Education through Assistive Technology. *T H E Journal* 30(7), pp. 24-30.

Blogging—A Tool for Education and Free Speech

Blogging, a term created from the word weblog, refers to the practice of creating or contributing to an online journal. Participants are sometimes called bloggers. The content of a blogger's journal addresses an issue of interest to the scribes who contribute. Entries are usually chronological and updated regularly.

Some Web sites host a number of blogging journals or sites. People interested in creating a blogging site must have a server on which to host the site or have a blogging account with a commercial site. Contributors sometimes use their real names in the journal, but often use aliases.

The form of the blogging journal is simple. Most include a list of responses to the primary blog subject or responses to comments made by other contributors.

When a user first sees a blogging journal, he or she may note that it looks somewhat similar to an Internet chat session with a number of threads from contributors. There are differences. The blogging journal, for example, because it is available to all on the Internet, is more accessible to a larger number of participants than newsgroup chat groups available only through individual Internet providers.

The blogging phenomenon has created and defined a unique community of Web users. The virtual community for blogging advocates is sometimes called a blogosphere. Many bloggers have found productive applications for the blog exchanges. For example, blogging can be used in education as a kind of Internet diary. The journal may be monitored by a teacher who may comment to the student about the quality of the reflection contained in the entries. Such usage encourages teachers to use blogging for the development of critical thinking and for the development of a writing voice.

Cybersins and Digital Good Deeds
© 2007 by The Haworth Press, Inc. All rights reserved.
doi:10.1300/5632_02

11

The significance of blogging as a tool for compiling opinions about topical issues is far reaching. Bloggers in the United States include prominent spokesmen who seek to solicit input on a wide array of topics including politics, the economy, legislative proposals, or social issues. The importance of blogging may be even more far reaching in countries outside the United States especially in countries that do not enjoy freedom of the press. For example, the capability of the unrestricted Internet to provide a person in China the opportunity to participate in a blogging site allows that person to exchange ideas in ways not available to him or her in the newspaper or on television.

BIBLIOGRAPHY

Kitzmann, A. (2003). That Different Place: Documenting the Self within Online Environments. *Biography* 26(1), pp. 48-66.

McNeill, L. (2003). Teaching an Old Genre New Tricks: The Diary on the Internet. *Biography* 26(1), pp. 24-48.

Oravec, J. A. (2002). Bookmarking the World: Weblog Applications in Education. *Journal of Adolescent & Adult Literacy* 45(7), pp. 616-621.

Stiler, G. M. and Philleo, T. (2003). Blogging and Blogspots: An Alternative Format for Encouraging Reflective Practice among Preservice Teachers. *Education* 123(4), pp. 789-797.

Bride Scams

Finding a mate by way of correspondence is hardly a new idea. Mail-order brides were not uncommon when America was in its early days and men greatly outnumbered women in unsettled parts of the country (Enss, 2005). In these times, potential brides were touted in newspaper advertisements, which evolved into slick photo albums as years passed. Today, like most other enterprises, the mail-order bride business has gone online in a big way.

Internet bride services are now international agencies that recruit their candidates from depressed areas worldwide and offer them to clients in America and other more affluent places. Eastern Europe and Southeast Asia are examples of regions from which thousands of women are enlisted. Often they are described as "traditional" wives who will be happy to be subservient spouses, less demanding and independent than Western women. On the surface, such arrangements may sound like win-win propositions. The husband gets a wife who is compatible with his desires and beliefs, and the wife gets a grateful husband, citizenship, and escape from an uncertain and limited future.

In reality, however, significant risks exist for both prospective spouses. Marriage brokers who arrange international matches work in a shadowy world with little regulation. Often one or both participants in a transaction may be greeted with unwelcome surprises. The young and often naïve bride may discover that the man she married but barely knew is an abuser. She may find herself in a strange place with no support system and nowhere to turn for help. The Tahirih Justice Center, an international women's rights group based in Virginia, asserts that domestic abuse in marriages arranged by international agencies is a growing problem (Briscoe, 2005).

The other side of the issue is when a hopeful husband ends up being victimized. The man who contracts with an agency may pay thousands of dollars in fees as well as the costs of bringing his new wife to his home. In a not-uncommon scenario, all may go well for a short time; then problems arise. The subservient bride turns out to be anything but. Conflict between the two escalates, leading to divorce. Looking back, the erstwhile husband realizes he was just a vehicle by which his "dream bride" obtained escape from her country and gained U.S. citizenship.

The old saying "caveat emptor," or "let the buyer beware," applies in matrimony as well as in other transactions. The chance of a happy ending carries along with it the possibility of a nightmarish outcome.

BIBLIOGRAPHY

Briscoe, D. (2005). Mail-Order Misery. *Newsweek* 145 (February 7), p. 54.

Enss, C. (2005). *Hearts West: True Stories of Mail-Order Brides on the Frontier.* Guilford, CT: Globe Pequot Press.

Camcorders, Surveillance, and Video Voyeurism

The growth of the Internet gave users the ability not only to exchange text, sound, or still images, but also to exchange live video. Small camcorders attached to an Internet computer allowed users to purchase inexpensive software providing the Internet user the ability to broadcast moving images live to the world.

The capability of a camcorder and relevant software to capture video images and to broadcast them quickly produced an array of services. Local and state governments began using camcorders to monitor those who run red lights or commit other traffic violations. Businesses also began using camcorders to monitor shoplifting.

Internet camcorder usage moved into homes and provided a number of services especially for surveillance. Camcorders came to be used for home security systems as well as monitoring devices for parents who wanted to watch the behavior of children as the children played or slept in other rooms.

Since the mid-1990s, camcorders in our society became commonplace and came to be accepted in certain public places. In other places, however, they were less acceptable. For example, camcorders began showing up in places where one would expect privacy, including public bathrooms and public dressing areas. Some states are considering legislation banning cameras for any reason in restrooms or dressing areas. The presence of a camcorder and the Internet also provides resources for voyeurs who typically take pictures of women who are unaware they are being photographed. The pictures and videos often make their way to the voyeur's Web site.

Some camcorder users develop Web sites that broadcast their activities twenty-four hours a day. Some of these sites include the capability of watching private behavior, including sex. In addition to use by private citizens, pornography distributors use camcorders for broad-

Cybersins and Digital Good Deeds
© 2007 by The Haworth Press, Inc. All rights reserved.
doi:10.1300/5632_03

In the mid-1990s, camcorders in our society became commonplace and came to be accepted in many public places. (*Source*: © iStockphoto.com/Ling, Johnathan, "Camera on Side of Building." Available at http://www.istockphoto .com.)

casting live or taped sex acts. The pornography distributors usually require fees for Internet users to watch the sexually oriented broadcasts.

BIBLIOGRAPHY

Calvert, C. (2000). *Voyeur Nation: Media, Privacy, and Peering in Modern Culture.* Boulder, CO: Westview Press.

Harper, J. (1998). "Childbirth Goes Live on the Internet." *The Washington Times* (June 17), p. 6.

Harper, J. (1998). "Cyberspectacle Raises Eyebrows, Questions." *The Washington Times* (July 15), p. 6.

Sardar, Z. (2000). The Rise of the Voyeur. *New Statesman* (November 6), p. 25.

Virulent Viewing or Picture Taking? (2003). *State Legislatures* (May), p. 9.

Cell Phone Rage

Cell phones are both a blessing and an anathema. It is a common occurrence to see people out and about, walking and talking on their cell phones. Whatever happened to enjoying one's surroundings? Why would a hiker want to be on his cell phone while enjoying incredible natural beauty on a beach or trail? Why don't people sitting together talk to each other instead of distant parties via phones? All this is well and good, if a little hard to figure, until the talkers infringe on the serenity of other people.

Who has not been annoyed by loud, one-sided conversations in restaurants, waiting rooms, and other public places? Even worse, calls may be argumentative or personal in nature, subjecting those unfortunate enough to be nearby to way too much information about the talker's life. In response to the problem, some restaurants offer "cell-free zones" or ban phones altogether, as do most libraries and some doctor's waiting rooms. But you still can be caught as a captive audience on public transportation, in lines, and in other public gathering places.

Just the ringing of the phone, often playing a poor rendition of a familiar song, can be extremely irritating. To make things worse, there are even intentionally obnoxious ring tones that people can buy to assign to users they want to avoid. A recent play in Israel was interrupted no less than ten times by ringing phones, and there is even a story of an undertaker's phone going off from a grave during a burial ceremony. According to Christine Rosen (2004), the Cingular cellular telephone company did a survey on powering down phones and found that southerners are more likely to turn off phones in church, and westerners are more likely to do so in libraries, theaters, restaurants, and schools. Cingular has gone on to promote the slogan "Be Sensible" and encourage people to use common sense about when and where to turn on phones or conduct conversations. In some instances, this warning has fallen on deaf ears and people have gotten into verbal and even physical altercations over rude cell phone use. But before you think about confronting an offensive cell phone user, think twice. There is also a device on the market that looks like a phone but is really a stun gun.

In early 2005 the FAA floated the idea of in-flight cell phone use, heretofore banned because such use could interfere with flight controls. It seems that experts now agree that this problem is overstated. Thus, says Andy Dornan (2005), passengers may be subjected to cell phone air pollution in one of the last bastions of silence, with the effects thereof yet to be seen. Many travelers are making it clear, though, that they do not like the idea of cell phones in the air. The majority of comments on the topic that have been sent to the FCC after announcing the possibility were negative. People said they do not want to have to listen to others' conversations while flying. Enough is enough, many say, when it comes to cell phone use in public spaces.

BIBLIOGRAPHY

Dornan, A. (2005). Who's Counting? *Network Magazine* 20 (July), pp. 1-3.

Rosen, C. (2004). Our Cell Phones, Ourselves, *The New Atlantis* 6 (Summer 2004), pp. 26-45.

Siegel, R. (2002). "Cell Phones are Becoming a Portable Source Capable of Broadcasting Personal Embarrassment," *All Things Considered, National Public Radio*, (April 4).

Cell Phones and Driving

Driving and talking on a cell phone is a dangerous combination. This may sound like an obvious statement, but surveys show that between 80 and 90 percent of cell phone users talk and drive, thus inspiring bumper stickers such as SHUT UP AND DRIVE and DRIVE NOW TALK LATER. According to Silva (2005), more than half of all Americans are cell phone owners, so the number of people conversing and driving along with you in traffic or on the highway is bound to be considerable at all times.

Perhaps you say, "I am not part of the problem because I only use my hands-free device behind the wheel." Studies strongly suggest that the problem is not only the location of a person's hands, but also what is going on inside his or her head. According to Pappalardo (2005), drivers using hands-free devices have still performed poorly in both simulated and real road tests when compared with drivers who do not have the distraction. Studies have even suggested that using a cell phone has a physiological effect on a person, causing a decrease in peripheral vision. The effect, called "inattention blindness," was akin to tunnel vision and occurred with both handheld and hands-free talkers. So if the person talking away in the car next to you appears dangerously distracted, he or she probably is.

The National Highway Traffic Safety Administration in 2003 called for restrictions to cell phone use at least for new drivers, including those with learner's provisional licenses, and intermediate permits (Ropeik and Gray, 2003). As of early 2005, two states had passed laws against cell phone use for all drivers—New York and California. Seventeen states had restrictions regarding novice drivers. In other instances, cities such as Chicago have passed local ordinances against talking and driving. Because of the possibility of lawsuits, certain companies are putting into place policies barring employees from driving and using cell phones while on the job. Such measures are met with strong opposition from companies selling the phones and services, but the trend toward regulation continues. Regardless of laws and policies, pulling over in a safe place to make calls is clearly the prudent course for the careful driver.

Surveys show that between 80 and 90 percent of cell phone users talk and drive despite evidence that it greatly increases risk of accidents. (*Source*: © iStock photo.com/Barskaya, Galina, "Driving." Available at http//:www.istockphoto.com.)

BIBLIOGRAPHY

Pappalardo, D. (2005). Keep Your Hands On the Wheel. *Network World* 13 (April 4), p. 42.

Ropeik, D. and Gray, G. (2003). Cell Phones and Driving: How Risky? *Consumer Research Magazine* 86 (January), pp. 14-16.

Silva, J. (2005). States Restrict Cell Phone Use for Teen Drivers. *RCR Wireless News* 24 (April 25), pp. 4-21.

Cell Yell

A new term entered our language with the ubiquitous presence of cell phones. *Cell yell* was coined to describe the tendency of many cell phone users to talk louder into their tiny devices, as if that were necessary in order to be heard by the person with whom they were talking. That, coupled with the fact that unwilling bystanders are thereby forced to hear only one half of someone else's conversation, causes even more annoyance than being party to a louder-than-necessary conversation in which all participants are present. Andrew Monk and

The phrase *cell yell* was coined to describe the tendency of many cell phone users to talk louder than necessary into their tiny devices, often inflicting their private conversations upon others in public places. (*Source:* © iStockphoto.com/ Sharon Dominick Photography, "Emotions-Male-Angry Call." Available at http//: www.istockphoto.com.)

colleagues from the University of York proved this in a series of staged interactions taking place on public transportation (Liberman, 2004). It seems that hearing only one side of a conversation that one would prefer not to hear at all is particularly frustrating. Often there is a self-important attitude exuded by the speaker, as if his business is so unique, important, and fascinating that surely others want to hear about it. As previously stated, such rude and thoughtless behavior should be curbed.

BIBLIOGRAPHY

Liberman, M. (2004). Mind Reading Experiments at the University of York's Language Lab. (April 13). Available at http://itre.cis.upenn.edu/~myl/languagelog.
Strand, E. (2005). Overheard—But Not Overjoyed. *Psychology Today* 38 (January/February), p. 34.

Censorship and Filtering

Censorship is an especially difficult issue for those such as public librarians who wish to provide quality Internet access without government regulations but are concerned about protecting users from pornography or threatening information. One option for providing protection involves using a hardware or software filter. The argument over censorship and filtering in public libraries has spilled over to public schools and to public school librarians who face similar issues as they provide Internet access to students.

Rich Chapin (1999) has addressed the issue by noting the importance of distinguishing by definition between censorship and filtering. According to Chapin, censorship is as an act performed by the government that restricts free speech assured in the constitution, whereas filtering is a means to keep students from accessing unsuitable Web sites.

Chapin's rationale in establishing a dichotomy between censorship as limiting Web site access by a government official and filtering as limiting Web site access by a teacher or librarian allows schools to move forward in providing Internet resources for instructional purposes. Censorship may deny a person free speech rights. Filtering involves ensuring access to appropriate instructional materials.

If a librarian chooses to use a filtering system for restricting Internet access, the capability of the filtering system may be important in allowing teachers or librarians to control the Internet experience and to do so in a way that best meets the curriculum needs of the students. Most systems keep a database of Web addresses that cannot be accessed by students; however, the better filtering systems allow teachers or librarians to add appropriate sites and to remove Web sites they feel are inappropriate.

BIBLIOGRAPHY

Bell, B. W. (2001). Filth, Filtering, and the First Amendment: Ruminations on Public Libraries' Use of Internet Filtering Software. *Federal Communications Law Journal* 53(2), p. 187.

Chapin, R. (1999). Content Management, Filtering and the World Wide Web. *T H E Journal* 27(2), p. 44.

Dyrli, O. E. (2001). Internet Filters: Good or Bad, Now Necessary. *Curriculum Administrator* (April), p. 33.

Lasica, J. D. (1997) Censorship Devices on the Internet. *American Journalism Review* (September), p. 56.

Semitsu, J. P. (2000). Burning Cyberbooks in Public Libraries: Internet Filtering Software vs. the First Amendment. *Stanford Law Review* 52(2), p. 509.

Simon, G. E. (1998). Cyberporn and Censorship: Constitutional Barriers to Preventing Access to Internet Pornography by Minors. *Journal of Criminal Law and Criminology* 88(3), pp. 1015-1048.

Cheating at School
Using Cell Phone Cameras

As productive instructional uses for technology became evident during the mid-1990s for students in elementary school through college, some uses emerged that allow students to acquire and share information improperly. A particularly vexing practice for educators occurs when students use technology to acquire and share information included on either a teacher's test or on a standardized test. Camera-equipped cell phones provide a new resource for those students who wish to go beyond accepted bounds to succeed. The fact that the camera is able not only to capture an image but also to share that image instantly to others gives the device a unique dimension in

Camera-equipped cell phones added the capability for a student to take a picture of text and to share that information with a test taker. Some school officials have limited their use.

acquiring information and getting that information into the hands of another.

Cheating practices usually fall into two categories. The first practice involves a student taking a picture of the test during an examination period, electronically sending that picture to someone who researches specific questions, and receiving the answers back via the cell phone. Another practice involves taking pictures of a test during an examination period and storing that information in the phone's memory so that the test may be shared with others scheduled to take the test at a later date.

Cheating with the use of camera-equipped cell phones is a practice that not only occurs in a regular classroom, but also occurs in standardized testing classrooms such as during the administration of the Scholastic Aptitude Test or the Graduate Record Examination. The proliferation of camera-equipped cell phones as a tool for cheating has created enough of a disturbance that many schools limit their use not only during testing sessions but during the regular school day as well.

BIBLIOGRAPHY

Cizek, G. J. (1999). *Cheating on Tests: How to Do It, Detect It, and Prevent It.* Mahwah, NJ: Lawrence Erlbaum Associates.
Should We Ban Cell Phones in School? (2004). *NEA Today* (February), p. 42.

Child Online Protection Act and Children's Online Privacy Protection Act

The Child Online Protection Act (COPA) came into being in 1998 as an attempt to block Internet pornography available to children. The bill required that commercial Web site developers provide protections so that harmful material could not be accessed by underage users. The standard for "harmful material" was based upon community standards. After its passage, COPA experienced immediate criticism as being too broad in using community standards as a criterion for defining "harmful." COPA was challenged in court and has never taken effect.

Critics of the bill focused on more than the constitutional issues raised by COPA. They also argued that inadequate government regulations would create complacency among parents who think that such regulations are fail safe. Other critics noted that COPA could prevent children from accessing proper information.

Because of the similarity of the acronyms, COPA is often confused with COPPA, the Children's Online Privacy Protection Act, a 1998 law requiring that Web sites accessed by children under thirteen must require parental consent for certain types of access. Parental consent also must be given in order for the child user to give his or her name or address. COPPA went into effect in 2000 and has not been challenged in court to date. One negative effect of COPPA is that it has forced some legitimate children's Web sites to go out of business because of the expense of compliance.

COPPA has raised some issues for school librarians and teachers who now have to consider their "in loco parentis" status in making the determination as to whether a student is able to access certain sites or provide personal information on the Internet.

BIBLIOGRAPHY

Davis, J. J. (2002). Marketing to Children Online: A Manager's Guide to the Children's Online Privacy Protection Act. *SAM Advanced Management Journal* 67(4), pp. 11-21.

Duin, J. (1998). "Bill Aims to Keep Children Away from Porn Web Sites." *The Washington Times* (May 11), p. 3.

Fahey, M. (2000). "CHILDREN'S INTERNET SAFETY NET: As More Youngsters Reap Benefits Offered on the World Wide Web, Parents Must Learn to Protect Them from an Array of Unsuitable Sites." *The Washington Times* 1 (August), p. 1.

Glanz, W. (1999). Child-Data Collection Restricted on Internet. *Insight on the News* (November 29), p. 27.

Glanz, W. (2000). "New Privacy Act Spurs Web Sites to Oust Children." *The Washington Times* (April 20), p. 1.

Gore, A., Jr. (2000). Digital Opportunity in the New Millennium: Making the Internet Work for All Americans. *Business Perspectives* (Spring), p. 2.

Hersh, Melanie L. (2001). Is COPPA a Cop out? The Child Online Privacy Protection Act as Proof That Parents, Not Government, Should Be Protecting Children's Interests on the Internet. *Fordham Urban Law Journal* 28(6), p. 1831.

Child Pornography
Prevention Act

The Child Pornography Prevention Act (CPPA), which was enacted in 1996 in an attempt to protect children from virtual pornography, expanded the definition of child pornography to include digital graphics that suggest the image of a child involved in sexual activity. The law focused on graphics, including both hard copy and digital, that were created on a computer as a picture that did not include the depiction of a real child but did include a computer-generated image of a child involved in sexually oriented activity.

Since CPPA addressed those developers who created such graphics, the impact of the law was primarily felt by commercial Web site developers. Most Internet users were not affected.

The law was challenged in regional appellate courts and later challenged in the Supreme Court, which struck down CPPA in April, 2002. Justice Kennedy writing for the majority noted that the CPPA failed to distinguish between pornography and digital images with artistic value and, as such, was too broad to be enforced.

BIBLIOGRAPHY

Lipschultz, J. H. (2000). *Free Expression in the Age of the Internet: Social and Legal Boundaries.* Boulder, CO: Westview Press.

Mota, S. A. (2002). The U.S. Supreme Court Addresses the Child Pornography Prevention Act and Child Online Protection Act in Ashcroft v. Free Speech Coalition and Ashcroft v. American Civil Liberties Union. *Federal Communications Law Journal* 55(1), pp. 85-98.

Rajala, J. (2002). Web Site Filtering. *T H E Journal* 30(5), p. 30.

Thornburgh, D. and Lin, H. (2004). Youth, Pornography, and the Internet: Although Technology and Public Policy Can Help, Social and Educational Strategies Are the Key to Protecting Children. *Issues in Science and Technology* 20(2) (Winter), pp. 43-48.

Wetzstein, C. (2000). "New Measure Takes Aim at Obscene Sites on Web." *The Washington Times* (December 24), p. 2.

Children's Internet Protection Act

The Children's Internet Protection Act (CIPA) became law on December 21, 2000, as an attempt to ensure that students are protected as they use the Internet in school. The law requires that schools provide Internet safety for the children they serve by providing practices, resources, and communications that define and explain the school's effort to limit what students access on the Internet. The law is aggressive in its enforcement. Schools not in compliance may have federal title and library monies withheld and may lose the privilege of buying discounted technology services.

The Internet Safety Policy required by CIPA outlines the procedures the school must create to ensure that students do not access inappropriate information. The Internet Safety Policy also defines the measures to be taken by the school to ensure the proper use of e-mail, to monitor chat rooms, to protect personal student information, and to prohibit access to computers by unauthorized users. Schools must hold at least one public hearing identifying the steps to be taken to provide Internet safety for students.

CIPA has been challenged in the Supreme Court by the American Library Association and the Freedom to Read Foundation; however, on June 23, 2003, the constitutionality of CIPA was upheld. Statements by individual Justices regarding the case did note concerns about the application of CIPA to adults.

BIBLIOGRAPHY

Rajala, J. (2002). Web Site Filtering. *T H E Journal* 30(5), p. 30.

Thornburgh, D. and Lin, H. (2004). Youth, Pornography, and the Internet: Although Technology and Public Policy Can Help, Social and Educational Strategies Are the Key to Protecting Children. *Issues in Science and Technology* (Winter), pp. 43-48.

Wetzstein, C. (2004). "New Measure Takes Aim at Oscene Sites on Web." *The Washington Times* (December 24), p. 2.

Willard, N. (2002). Complying with Federal Law for Safe Internet Use. *School Administrator* (April), p. 30.

Computer Addiction

As early as the late 1980s, well before the widespread use of the Internet, psychologists were voicing concerns about a new phenomenon involving obsessive use of computers. In 1989 M. A. Shotten wrote about compulsive behaviors displayed by a relatively small group of men who worked developing computer hardware and software in her book *Computer Addiction? A Study of Computer Dependency.* Her contention was that their fascination with computers interfered with their normal life and relationships. Perhaps her observations were prophetic, because concern regarding the disorder has grown incrementally since that time.

In the early days, compulsive behaviors centered on activities such as playing games, using popular software, or arranging files. As the Internet became more and more ubiquitous, it offered additional activities for the avid user. Although a certain amount of skepticism exists about the reality of this disorder, it seems to be gaining acceptance from professionals as a real psychological disorder. As pointed out by Orzack (1998), it is hard to define the malady since no one has a clear definition of normal or healthy computer use. However, certain symptoms have been cited as red flags, including

- neglecting family and other relationships in favor of computer use;
- experiencing symptoms such as restlessness or irritability when denied use;
- lying to other people about the extent of one's computer use;
- failing at efforts to cut back or control use;
- continuing despite physical complaints such as carpal tunnel syndrome, migraine, etc;
- neglecting work, studies, or other necessary activities in favor of use; and
- continuing to use the computer even in the face of damage to relationships, jobs, or other facets of life.

People get hooked on computer use for a number of reasons. Some people are attracted to the excitement of assuming a new identity, some report that computing is relaxing to them, and some turn to the Internet to escape reality. People with low self-esteem are especially vulnerable. Other lures include pornography, Internet gambling, and online shopping. Treatment for computer addiction is therefore a complex challenge, but many psychologists believe that cognitive behavior therapy and group therapy are positive approaches.

BIBLIOGRAPHY

Katz, W. (2002). *Introduction to Reference Work, Vol. II.* New York: McGraw-Hill.

Mitchell, P. (2000). Internet Addiction: Genuine Diagnosis or Not? *The Lancet* 365 (February 19), p. 632.

Orzack M. (1998). Computer Addiction, What Is It? *Psychiatric Times* 15 (August). Available at http://www.psychiatrictimes.com. Accessed July 16, 2006.

Orzack, M. (2005). Computer addiction services. Available at http://www.computeraddiction.com. Accessed July 16, 2006.

Computer Security

Practicing good computer security, whether it's protecting servers that contain sensitive customer data or personal computers that include identification information, personal documents, and possibly even financial records, is extremely important. The most basic method of securing a computer is to physically lock it up. Although computer hardware costs are decreasing, the technology is not so inexpensive as to leave it vulnerable to theft. Protecting the contents of a computer's hard drive is critical, as evidenced by the May 2006 theft of a Department of Veterans Affairs laptop computer that contained the personal information of 26.5 million veterans and active-duty service members (Yen, 2006). Although the laptop was recovered by the FBI the following month, amid claims by the bureau's security experts that the data was not accessed, there's still no 100 percent guarantee that the data was protected from misuse.

One security aspect that many computer users rarely use is password protection. Passwords can be used to lock individual files, folders, or even the operating system of a computer. Passwords are best when they are alphanumeric, that is, a combination of letters and numbers: "h3llo," for example. An even better method is to use an alphanumeric passphrase, or combination of words and numbers: "w3h0ldth3s3truths." Although this can become complicated to type, it makes the system or file much more difficult to crack.

In addition to using passwords or passphrases, users should also keep their operating system security up to date through official updates and patches (small fixes for previously released software). Newer versions of Mac and Windows operating systems have automatic updates set as the default, allowing systems to download and install content automatically or by prompt. Some distributions of the Linux operating system offer automatic updates as well.

Commercial products, such as Norton Internet Security and McAfee Internet Security Suite, can also be used to bolster a computer's defenses. In addition to providing anti-virus, anti-hacker, and firewall protection (a firewall is a software or hardware barrier that filters traffic in and out of a computer), such programs can also defend against spyware—software that is surreptitiously installed on a computer, which monitors and collects information about a user. Spyware is often used by advertising agencies to analyze browsing habits and customize ads, and malicious versions can even be used by hackers to intercept passwords and financial information, such as credit card and bank account numbers (Wikipedia.org).

Hackers, crackers, and other computer and Internet thieves are continually updating their methods of attack. Therefore it is in users' best interest to keep their systems up to date with the latest security software, and to protect their computers both physically and electronically from exploitation and misuse.

BIBLIOGRAPHY

Wikipedia.org. Spyware. Available at http://en.wikipedia.org/wiki/Spyware. Accessed July 28, 2006.

Yen, H. (2006). FBI Says Data on VA Laptop Not Accessed. Available at http://www.cbsnews.com/stories/2006/06/29/ap/politics/mainD8II3ESG0.shtml?CMP = ILC-SearchStories. Accessed July 21, 2006.

Crackers, Lamers, and Phreaks

All social groups have hierarchies; technology groups are not different. We are all familiar with hackers. This term itself has transferred meaning from negative to positive. In fact, much of the free, open-source software available on the Internet has been hacked to make it better for users. However, there are a few other delineations that will be covered here.

Lamers are users who have poor typing skills or overuse emoticons in chat. The term is also applied to users with no respect for authority or convention in the context of using some communication facility, as well as to those with any variety of behaviors that are thought to be annoying. Script kiddies (see pages 137-138) are often called lamers or crackers.

Crackers are those who maliciously break into security systems, though usually with low-level expertise. According to Wikipedia.org, the term was coined by programmer and acclaimed hacker Richard Stallman as an alternative to using hacker for this meaning. Crackers are also those who break copy protection of software. Another type of cracking is phreaking, in which a communications network is broken into (see page 129).

BIBLIOGRAPHY

Wikipedia.org. Security Cracking. Available at http://en.wikipedia.org/wiki/Cracker%28computing%29. Accessed June 13, 2006.

Creating an Identity in a Chat Room

Internet chat rooms offer a unique opportunity for users to engage in text exchange with another person. When participating in the chat, participants often have the opportunity to create a bogus user name allowing the users to participate anonymously.

During a chat exchange, the user may use descriptive, suggestive, or intimate rhetoric that gives the exchange some of the feel of a face-to-face encounter. When this happens, the chat may, for some users, fill the need for a meaningful and fulfilling relationship.

The digital intimacy provided in a chat room may allow the encounter to develop into an exchange of sexual comments with participants playing different roles. Adopting a specific role affords users the opportunity to experience some degree of sexual gratification as a result of the exchange. Participating in Internet chat rooms may, in effect, allow technology to play a role in satisfying human instincts and may do so in ways that border between fantasy and reality.

The format of the sexual exchanges during a chat may look like an evolving script that moves from personal statements, to suggestive statements, to fantasy foreplay, and finally to statements suggesting different types of sexual activity that could occur should the participants ever meet. The chat exchanges may culminate with the end of the session or, in some instances, a user may suggest physical meetings between participants.

Physical meetings that occur as a result of a chat exchange can become an especially grim affair when a pedophile or other sexual predator uses a chat room to find victims and to propose meetings. Parental monitoring of chat rooms must become a crucial parental responsibility as children may find in a chat room a person they feel is reaching out to them in a special and positive way when in fact they have found a predator.

BIBLIOGRAPHY

Griffiths, M. (2001). Sex on the Internet: Observations and Implications for Internet Sex Addiction. *The Journal of Sex Research* 38(4), pp. 333-351.

Malkin, M. (2000). Parental Neglect Leads Teenagers to Be Seduced on the Internet. *Insight on the News* (June 5), p. 46.

Marshall, J. (2003). The Sexual Life of Cyber-Savants. *The Australian Journal of Anthropology* 14(2), pp. 229-248.

Thompson, N. (2000). Sex in the Digital City. *Washington Monthly* (July), p. 27.

Wetzstein, C. (2000). Chat Rooms Breed Disease. *Insight on the News* (September 4), p. 31.

Cyberbullying

At one time bullies were confined to relatively small arenas, such as the playground, neighborhood, or work place. In such an area, a bully could make life miserable for those who were vulnerable to attack. This still goes on, of course, and is a continuing problem which can lead to serious and violent acts on the part of the bully or as retaliation from a victim who finally fights back. This cycle has gained notoriety as a cause of school and even workplace violence.

Today bullying has gone online with frequent incidents ranging from teasing to stalking. Cyberbullies use e-mail, instant messaging, and cell phone or pager text messaging to harass, humiliate, and threaten targets. They also create defamatory Web pages or use free Web communities and polling sites to post cruel questionnaires about their victims. This kind of behavior is common in schools all over the world. Examples include an overweight Japanese boy who was photographed with a cell phone camera while changing clothes for gym class. According to Amanda Paulson (2003), a middle-schooler in Canada found herself ostracized after someone phoned around a rumor that she had been exposed to SARS. Also in Canada, a teenage boy, playing at home with his new video camera, filmed himself reenacting a Star Wars laser sword fight scene. The tape was swiped by "friends" who uploaded it to the Internet. Soon he was an international object of ridicule known as the Star Wars Kid. The experience, says Paulson (2003), was enough to cause him to drop out of school and send him into counseling. His parents filed suit against the instigators, but the damage was done.

Many times kids who might not publicly harass someone find it easy to do anonymously while sitting at a computer. A 2000 poll shows that 17 million teenagers used AOL's instant messenger at that time. According to a Pew study, teens often find IM an easier way to say things that they would not say face to face, and that includes putdowns and slams. A 2002 survey by NCH, a British children's charity, reported that one in four students there had been bullied online (Paulson, 2003).

Cyberbullying can extend beyond brief IMs or text messages. Sometimes photographs are weapons of choice with a little help from editing software. In one instance an overweight girl was featured on a Web site with her head joined to the body of a cow (Paulson, 2003). Kids may also post entire sites defaming other youngsters, questioning their sexual orientations, and conducting polls with questions such as "Who is the ugliest kid at your school?" Online communities such as Xanga are especially popular for these types of postings.

The problem of cyberbullying needs to be addressed by adults on two fronts. Nancy Willard (2005), Oregon lawyer and proponent of safe Internet use, offers guidelines for both parents and educators. First, parents and guardians should be on the lookout for signs of problems at home. They should be aware of the potential for this sort of problem, and know how their children are interacting with others via the Internet. Parents of victims and bullies alike should be proactive and watchful for participation by their children. Second, schools recognize that cyberbullying is not something they can ignore, even if it occurs off campus. They must have and enforce policies that prohibit such behavior that spills over into the school environment, hampering students' abilities to work together and learn. Although school officials may be limited in their abilities to respond to off campus communications, they should not simply ignore what is happening. They should educate students, offer support to victims, and be ready to step in when the activities spill over into the schools.

In the days before Internet communication, victims of bullies could escape their harassers and find comfort at home. Now they are likely to leave a painful atmosphere at school or work only to be victimized once more at home when they log on their computers or use their cell phones. Students, parents, and educators need to understand the seriousness of this problem and take steps to deal with it.

BIBLIOGRAPHY

Beckerman, L. and Nocero, J. (2003). High-Tech Student Hate Mail. *Education Digest* 6 (February), p. 37.

Blair, J. (2003). New Breed of Bullies Torment Their Peers on the Internet. *Education Week* 22 (February 5), pp. 6-9.

Paulson, A. (2003). Internet Bullying. *Christian Science Monitor* 96 (December 30), p. 1C.

Willard, N. (2000). Choosing Not to Go Down the Not-So-Good Cyberstreets. *Center for Safe and Responsible Internet Use* (December 13). Available at http://cyberbully.org. Accessed July 16, 2006.

Cyberchondriacs

Medical information available via the Internet may be a boon to many, but it can lead to problems as well. For one thing, it can accentuate hypochondria, the tendency to worry excessively about real or imagined maladies and threats to one's health. Prior to the emergence of the Internet, hypochondriacs were prone to scanning print resources for health information or to repeatedly consulting their doctors. Now they can access a plethora of possible explanations for all imaginable symptoms. To further exacerbate the situation, much of what they find is apt to be inaccurate and possibly downright quackery. Even authoritative information may not be applicable or appropriate, and certainly this is true if the seeker suffers from hypochondria. According to Griffin (2002), one woman searched the Internet for floaters, those annoying little black dots that everyone sees from time to time. Generally these little specks do not indicate a serious medical condition, but she learned that they can be an early symptom of multiple sclerosis (MS). At that point her imagination took over, and she became convinced that she was afflicted with MS. As a result of her fears, her life was drastically affected. The obvious solution is to get a "live" medical checkup, but for some people this is not enough. Cyberchondriacs often second-guess their doctors when they get reassuring reports about their health. In such cases, the individual needs treatment for hypochondria itself, which may include counseling and medication for anxiety.

As for less compulsive users of medical information found on the Internet, it is important to remember that such data may be helpful and enlightening but should not always be accepted at face value. Internet sites should be closely scrutinized for authority, and doctors should be consulted for definitive health diagnoses and information.

BIBLIOGRAPHY

Griffin, R. M. (2002). Cyberchondria. *Web MD* (September 23). Available at http://my.webmd.com/Article/40407.htm. Accessed July 16, 2006.

Disinformation

According to the Merriam-Webster Online Dictionary, misinformation is simply incorrect information, whereas disinformation is inaccurate information presented with the intentional purpose of being misleading. Both abound on the Internet. The practice of scamming or deceiving people through advertising, news releases, political publications, etc., is nothing new. Purveyors of dubious medicinal remedies, overzealous campaign operatives, and biased news reporters have been around as long as the printed word. Today, however, with the wide open Internet, the "art" of disinformation has risen to new heights. One recent fertile field for disinformation was the 2004 U.S. presidential campaign. From the Swift Boat Veterans for Truth to the famous Dan Rather inquiry into President George W. Bush's military records, both ends of the political spectrum presented their versions of "truth" offered up with considerable spin. Dissembling is not limited to politics. Internet ads, conveniently showing up as spam in our e-mail, tout the wonders of countless questionable cures to fix everything from sexual dysfunction of obesity. News reporting is even less reliable than ever, thanks to the likes of Jayson Blair, the *New York Times* reporter who falsified sources and information.

What should be done in the face of rampant spin, hype, and general hokum? Journalists and schools of journalism should redouble efforts to stick to the ethical standards they purport themselves to endorse. Far more important, the general public needs to understand the importance of critically evaluating information. A 2005 Pew study found that Internet searchers are far less critical than they should be (Miller, 2005). By and large most people are satisfied to use just one search tool, probably Google, and then accept whatever it serves up. Internet users should try to discern the validity of Web sites by considering authority, currency, bias, and other factors. In addition, several Web-based entities can assist in evaluating information. Fact Check (http://www.factcheck.org) is a very well-known organization

Cybersins and Digital Good Deeds
© 2007 by The Haworth Press, Inc. All rights reserved.
doi:10.1300/5632_04

that seeks to line up political statements with underlying facts. Snopes (http://www.snopes.com) is great for debunking Internet hoaxes, including false political claims. Until people are discerning enough to look closely at the information that is obtained so easily via the Internet, those who seek to deceive through disinformation will thrive.

BIBLIOGRAPHY

Grimm, M. (2004) Tools of Disinformation. *Brandweek* 45 (September 6), pp. 17-20.
Miller, N. (2005). Anti-Spin: Using Internet Resources to Unwind Political Claims. *ETC: A Review of General Semantics* 62 (January), p. 76.

Disinhibition

For many people, online communication is a major or even sole reason for using the Internet. E-mail use is the entry point for many who have a bit of anxiety about trying to use computer technology for the first time. It is wonderful to be able to keep up with family and friends around the country and world via e-mail. In addition to e-mail, users can communicate through message boards, blogs, instant messaging, and live chat. They can even see their loved ones if they are using webcams. All of these relatively new and continually developing ways of keeping in touch are changing the way people communicate.

In many ways, this is all to the good. Sometimes people who have trouble communicating face to face or in social settings may find it less daunting to communicate online. A person who normally is uncomfortable expressing fears and wishes verbally may be able to do so online, thus enriching his or her own life and improving relationships.

As with many aspects of technology, though, the tendency for some people to "loosen up" online can have less salutary effects. Thus as participants in online conversations, we are likely to see angry outbursts, rude comments, and even threats in some online environments. These may come from people who would be far less apt to address others face to face in such fashion. People may also visit Internet sites such as hate or pornography pages, who would never publicly seek out such environments or groups in real life. A major reason for uncharacteristic behavior is anonymity. Online one can visit unsavory sites in the privacy of home with a fair degree of confidence that others will not know. It is also easy to invent an e-mail or chat name and persona that reveals nothing about one's true identity.

The clinical term for changed behavior resulting from the anonymous nature of the Internet use is *online disinhibition effect.* People on the net can dissociate themselves from their actions and words. They are free from the restricting boundaries of worrying about what others may think about their words and deeds. The faceless nature of most online communication means that one does not see the effect of words via facial expressions or body language. Because much communication is asynchronous, a person can "say" something at one time that will not be read until later, thus doing away with the need to deal with immediate reactions from recipients. The anonymity also gives rise to misunderstandings. What one person thought another was saying may be quite different from the original intent, especially if a person is being facetious or speaking tongue-in-cheek.

The effects of disinhibition should be clearly explained to young people and new Internet users. Online predators take advantage of the naiveté of youngsters far too often. Also, children and teens need to learn the potentially negative effects of their own Internet behavior. It is fine to develop an imaginary persona for a computer game, for instance, but it is not all right to mislead others by lying online or misrepresenting oneself to others in chat rooms or bulletin boards.

The online disinhibition effect is here to stay. As we communicate more and more via computers, handheld devices, cell phones and other electronic means, we need to take care that our own behavior meets our ethical standards and that we express ourselves clearly. Further, we must understand that others find online communication far too easy and tempting a means of misrepresenting themselves.

BIBLIOGRAPHY

Suler, J. (2004). The online disinhibition effect. *CyberPsychology and Behavior* 7 (June 1), pp. 321-326.

Distance Learning Content Sharing

An open-source digital graphical knowledge management system is the foundation for original and collaborative faculty content development for distance learning. Digital libraries are online information environments offering access to an assortment of resources and information services. As with traditional libraries, digital libraries attempt to develop and organize collections and services into a useful integrated environment. Digital libraries are not single entities; rather, digital libraries allow many transparent linkages to many other digital libraries providing universal access to information and document collections, including digital items that cannot be displayed or distributed on paper (e.g., audio and video). Digital libraries not only mediate between diverse and distributed information, but also the changing range of user communities. In this, digital libraries are less known for their holdings than their access to networked online environments. Consequently, we can think in terms of one all-encompassing library where patrons have access all the time, everywhere, on any device. Using digital libraries as a model, the system will offer creation, classification, dissemination, diffusion, utilization, and storage of knowledge. This knowledge will be the product of faculty research and collaboration. The system is a natural extension of research collaboration and authority of information created at the university level. The users and facilitators of this system will be faculty, staff, students, librarians, and technical staff. Through this system, users will have anytime, anywhere access to reliable data toward further research, content for traditional and distance learning courses, and electronic publication comprised of text, still images and graphics, audio, and video stored in a visual, spatial, relational database on any device. Once the system is in place, users need to understand how to use it. Users will require education in thinking about the system to best utilize it for their purposes. The users will also need training in the functionality of the system, how to enter and retrieve data, how to properly assign keywords to the document, and how to collaborate with others through the system. This will take a great deal of time at the outset, but will be a good investment toward the success of the system. Once users have the knowledge and skills to use this powerful tool, they will find great worth in exploiting it in all of their research and creative endeavors.

BIBLIOGRAPHY

Fox, E. A. (Ed.). (1995). *Source Book on Digital Libraries*. Blacksburg, VA: Virginia Tech.

Peters, T. A. (2000). Introduction. *Library Trends* 49(2) (Fall), pp. 221-227.

Bell, M. A., et al. (2004). Cybrarian. *Internet and Personal Computing Fads*. Binghamton, NY: Haworth Press, pp. 44-45.

Distributed Computing

Distributed computing is an excellent example of a technology good deed. Computer power is very rarely used to its fullest potential, both in task and processing time. In fact, most of our computers sit around collecting dust. Now computer users with an Internet connection can donate unused computer time and processing to the analysis of data. After downloading a screensaver or software agent, the software detects when the computer is online and uses the idle resources. Two popular examples of this technology are Grid.org, a site for large-scale research projects such as cancer, anthrax, and smallpox research, and seti@home, a site that uses Internet-connected computers to search for extraterrestrial intelligence.

By utilizing the usually limited personal computer power and adding the thousands to millions of other personal computing devices, a rather powerful virtual "supercomputer" is created. Put in real supercomputer terms, IBM's ASCI White, 2002's[1] most powerful computer is rated at 12 teraflops (one trillion floating-point operations per second) and cost $110 million, while the seti@home project averages about 15 teraflops and has cost only $500,000 so far, not to mention the costs of electrical power requirements, environmental controls (cold rooms), and similar recurring expenses.

NOTE

1. IBM's Blue Gene has topped 360 teraflops. Available at http://domino.research .ibm.com/comm/research_projects.nsf/pages/bluegene.index.html. Accessed July 21, 2006.

BIBLIOGRAPHY

Erlanger, L. (2002). Distributed Computing: An Introduction. *Extreme Tech* (April 4). Available at http://www.extremetech.com/article2/0,1697,11769,00.asp. Accessed July 21, 2006.
Grid.org. Available at http://www.grid.org/home.htm. Accessed July 21, 2006.
SETI@home. Available at http://setiathome.ssl.berkeley.edu. Accessed July 21, 2006.

Doctor-Patient Relationships

There once was a time when, for most people, the primary and even sole source of medical advice and information was the family doctor. Other alternatives might include home cures and word of mouth, but the mantle of authority rested on the shoulders of the doctor. Many people would accept diagnoses and recommendations uncritically, not even thinking of a second opinion, much less personal research. Trust in the doctor's infallibility may not have been blind, but it was substantial.

All that has changed in recent years, for a number of reasons. Patients and doctors are more mobile; referrals to specialists have increased, and managed care plans have sent patrons to doctors not previously known by them. Furthermore, the Internet has greatly affected the way people obtain medical information, and in the future will increasingly influence the way patients and doctors communicate. What does this situation have to do with cyberethics? Doctors and patients both must be responsible today for their roles in seeing that they keep up with the changing nature of their relationships. They must work together to provide and obtain the best possible medical care.

Patients should learn to avail themselves of the array of excellent Web sites that provide authoritative and valuable information. Hospitals offer resources for learning and support. Medical journals and other online resources provide opportunities for people to educate themselves. Web sites can provide information about physicians that may help future patients get to know them. At the same time, though, even more sites lack authority and contain biased information, misinformation, and downright quackery. Medications can be bought with nothing more than a credit card number and a few keystrokes. People desperate for relief, cure, or diagnosis are vulnerable to advertisements that may offer useless or even harmful alternatives to responsible medical practice. All this, both the good and the bad, is available without the patient ever leaving home or speaking to a physician. Individuals who turn to the Internet for advice, support, and information are wise to do so, but must be very critical and discerning. They must evaluate the sites they use with respect to authority, validity, currency, and bias. They must also learn to differentiate between information and promotion for profit.

Doctors have had to change their views of the doctor-patient relationship as well. Gone are they days when the doctor could "play God." A 2002 Pew Internet and American Life study showed that on any given day more people use the Internet for medical advice than actually visit health professionals (Redwood, 2006). Doctors are meeting patients who expect to be partners in their health care. The ethical doctor will view this increased desire on the part of patients to educate themselves as a positive thing, and will advise them about authoritative sources of information. More and more doctors and hospitals are increasing their own online presences, reaching out to people with reliable advice and information.

Thus while it may be true that the Internet can have a negative effect on people's health because of the amount of misinformation offered, that certainly does not have to be the case. The doctor-patient relationship can be improved as both parties work together, availing

The doctor-patient relationship can be improved as both parties work together, availing themselves of the Internet's ability to enhance communication and learning. (*Source:* © iStockphoto.com/Wisniewska, Monika, "Doctor and Patient." Available at http//:www.istockphoto.com.)

themselves of the Internet's ability to enhance communication and learning.

BIBLIOGRAPHY

Redwood, H. (2002). Patients, Doctors and the Internet: A Question of Trust. *Health and Age* (November 20). Available at http://www.healthandage.com. Accessed July 16, 2006.

Domain Hijacking

Domain hijacking is just that—taking over domain names illegally. Anyone who uses the Internet uses domains. Domain names are, essentially, labels of Internet addresses. For example, distance .shsu.edu comprises a subdomain (distance) of the shsu.edu domain name of the top-level domain .edu. Domain hijacking can disrupt or severely impact the business and operations of a domain owner, including the denial and theft of electronic mail services, unauthorized disclosure of information through phishing Web sites and eavesdropping, as well as Web site defacement. Domain name hijackers can replace financial institution Web sites with their own authentication portals and use these to collect user accounts and passwords. With this stolen account information, hijackers can withdraw and transfer funds, steal identities, and make online purchases. Also, by modifying a domain name server configuration, attackers are able to redirect e-mail, Internet protocol telephony, and electronic messenger conversations for an entire domain to their own systems.

Most computer security institutions recommend the following steps to protect against domain hijacking:

1. Keep track of domain names' expiration dates and keep contact information current;
2. Be aware of who is listed in domain contact information;
3. Be careful of using free e-mail addresses from services such as Yahoo or Hotmail. Free e-mail services usually suspend or delete an e-mail account if it is not logged into frequently;
4. Do not reply (or click on any links) in any domain related e-mail correspondence that is not recognized;
5. Add the registrar's domain name to your spam filter's approved sender list. If the registrant or Internet service provider is using a spam-blocking service, there is the risk of not receiving domain renewal notices from the registrar;

6. Consider renewing the domain name early and for a longer period of time; and
7. Routinely check the Whois service for current domain registration information.

BIBLIOGRAPHY

ICANN SSAC Releases Domain Name Hijacking Report. Available at http://www.icann.org/announcements/hijacking-report-12jul05.pdf . Accessed July 21, 2006.

DRM

DRM, or Digital Rights Management, refers to the method of protecting and securely delivering digital content to a technology device. This digital content includes music, video, and still images. The technology is used to hinder illegal duplication of media creating a revenue loss for content creators and publishers. Apple iTunes users will be familiar with this concept. After a customer purchases music from the iTunes Music Store, he or she is able to download the tracks to the computer where iTunes resides. The license agreement allows the music to be burned to a CD three times and kept on three different computers where that person's account is activated. This does not allow for sharing with others; the idea is that individuals have multiple computers.

The issues of DRM are those of copyright. According to Jessica Litman (2001), "the controversy over Internet piracy is a subplot to a much larger drama." The battle is more of how users may own and share digital media. As more personal media is created and shared as participation in culture, major entertainment companies seek to control all uses and reuses of their works at the expense of traditional rights.

It is interesting that the multibillion dollar entertainment industry has so much more influence than the multitrillion dollar technology industry. It is also interesting that media companies have not learned from past arguments against technology innovations. For example, Disney was a huge opponent of the VCR, in fact spending large sums to fight its development and delivery. After the company discovered that it could now rerelease all of its feature films, shorts, and the like on VHS, it made significant amounts of money on projects that may have well sat on a literal shelf collecting dust. In 2001, Disney Channel's animated series *The Proud Family* aired an episode in which Penny Proud becomes addicted to file sharing and begins downloading all of the music she has ever wanted to the detriment of her favorite singer, who doesn't get a royalty check, and the record store, which goes out of business. The police threaten to take her to jail, and her mom takes away her computer. She all but destroys the U.S. economy.

Signed by President Clinton on October 28, 1998, the Digital Millennium Copyright Act incorporates two key provisions, including the Internet service provider safe harbor, which frees ISPs from liability when copyrighted material pass through their systems, and the anti-circumvention provision, which made it illegal to manufacture, import, offer to the public, provide, or otherwise traffic in any technology designed to circumvent copy or access protection.

Many technology companies, including Apple, Microsoft, and TiVo, have also been including DRM in their products. As with any regulation, users are typically okay with DRM as long as their rights are fair.

BIBLIOGRAPHY

Lasica, J.D. (2005). *Darknet: Hollywood's War Against the Digital Generation.* Hoboken, NJ: John Wiley and Sons.

Litman, J. (2001). *Digital Copyright: Protecting Intellectual Property on the Internet.* Amherst, NY: Prometheus Books.

eBay and Online Auction Fraud

Online auctions hosted by eBay and other Web companies have become a popular way to sell and purchase items. Auctions have gained in popularity, and with the growth of online auctions, several types of fraudulent practices have emerged. The practices involve activities occurring either during or after the bidding process and may involve collaboration between a seller and a fake bidder or between two bidders.

The fraudulent practice between the seller and the fake bidder involves the fake bidder submitting a bid aimed at running up the price. The practice encourages bidders who are not aware of the scheme to increase their bids, thus benefiting the seller. On occasion, the person running up the bid may be the seller himself using a fake identity.

Other types of fraud involve collaborating bidders who work together to purchase an item for a small bid. The fraudulent act happens like this. If a bidder notes that there is a particularly small bid for an item, for example ten dollars, he may inject a high bid such as $1,000. This high bid discourages others from bidding as they do not wish to bid more than $1,000. Just before the auction is over, the high bidder withdraws his bid allowing the low bidder to buy the item for the small price of only ten dollars.

Other types of fraud occur after the auction is completed and may involve either the seller or the bidder. The most common fraud occurs when the winning bidder sends money to the seller and the seller does not send the merchandise or sends merchandise of a lesser quality than that advertised in the bid information. The bidder may also commit fraud by not sending the funds for an item that he or she has received.

The Federal Trade Commission has made an effort to make sellers and purchasers aware of online fraud strategies, and the awareness has improved confidence in online monetary exchanges for a commodity. Online auctions, however, still have their risk.

Cybersins and Digital Good Deeds
© 2007 by The Haworth Press, Inc. All rights reserved.
doi:10.1300/5632_05

BIBLIOGRAPHY

Albert, M. R. (2002). E-Buyer Beware: Why Online Auction Fraud Should Be Regulated. *American Business Law Journal* 39(4), pp. 575-643.

"Going, Going, Gone: Thousands Lose Big Money to Online Auction Fraud." (2002). *The Washington Times* (October 21), p. A01.

Snyder, J. M. (2000). Online Auction Fraud: Are the Auction Houses Doing All They Should or Could to Stop Online Fraud? *Federal Communications Law Journal* 52(2), p. 453.

Stefanova, K. (2000). Cyber Con Men Beware! *Insight on the News* (April 17), p. 27.

Elder Care and Technology

As today's baby boomers age, there is a growing interest in positive uses of technology in elder care, both for generation members' parents and for their present and future personal needs. By the year 2050 the percentage of the world's population over the age of sixty is projected to increase from the present 10 percent to twice that number. Included in this population will be a rapidly growing segment of individuals eighty-five or older (Home Alone, 2005).

Assistive technologies can play important roles in improving care and quality of life for people in their later years. One simple device that is gaining popularity is the talking medicine dispenser. By pressing a button on the bottom of a talking pill bottle, a user can hear a playback of prescription information as well as how many times per day the bottle has been opened. Cell phones and PDAs are also in the works to serve as memory aids and organizers. As more elderly people become comfortable with cell phones, transitioning to such devices will be relatively simple and can relieve nagging concerns about remembering things.

Today many elderly and disabled people wear devices that allow them to signal for help in the event of a fall or other emergency. Some wearable devices can also monitor a user's heart activity and other vital signs through wireless sensors. Going a step beyond this, systems are being developed that can follow a person's movements in his or her environment. Motion detectors throughout the abode will be able to send reports to an Internet site where a caregiver can virtually check in on a loved one or client and make sure that the person is going about his or her normal daily routine. Needless to say, such close monitoring of a person's daily life may raise concerns about privacy. Does Grandpa really want someone else to know how many times he opened the refrigerator or went out into the backyard? Proponents say the trade-offs are being able to live at home rather than in managed care, and allowing family members to have less concern about how a loved one is getting along on a day-to-day basis. Without a doubt the ways that technology can help older adults and their families will continue to evolve and offer alternatives to present elder care practices.

BIBLIOGRAPHY

Home Alone. (2005). *The Economist* 375 (June 11), pp. 8-9.

Pollack, M. (2005). Intelligent Intelligent Technology for an Aging Population: The Use of AI to Assist Elders with Cognitive Impairment. *AI Magazine* 2 (Summer), pp. 9-24.

Sterns, A. and Collins, S. (2005). Transforming the Personal Digital Assistant into a Health-Enhancing Technology. *Generations* 28 (Winter), pp. 54-56.

E-Mail Addresses and Privacy

The spread of e-mail throughout the United States and the world has increased dramatically during the past decade. The number of e-mail users with individual e-mail addresses provides a potential for contact between peoples in ways never dreamed of in the past. Yet this potential possesses a negative side in that e-mail addresses, once accessed by another, allow a user to receive unwanted and unsolicited e-mail messages.

E-mail addresses may be obtained in a number of ways. For example, if a user has his or her e-mail address in a browser configuration, that information can be read when the user goes to specific sites. In addition hackers may access e-mail addresses from remote sites, and network administrators may access them from other points on a network.

E-mail addresses can also be unknowingly provided by the legitimate owner of the e-mail account. This occurs when a user willingly shares his or her e-mail address during a business transaction not knowing that the recipient is saving the data to share with others. After the e-mail address is made available to another person, the address may be shared with groups, including businesses. The user then may begin receiving frequent unsolicited messages.

The implications for e-mail account use by unauthorized persons are even more critical when e-mail users choose simple passwords that can be easily figured out by others. In such cases, the e-mail address may then be used with the password to access financial information or to create new fraudulent financial accounts.

BIBLIOGRAPHY

Bourquard, J., Greenberg, P., and Boerner, R. D. (2000). America Is Online, and There's No Turning Back. *State Legislatures* (June), p. 26.

Brenowitz, S. (2000). Security.edu. *Matrix: The Magazine for Leaders in Higher Education* (September), p. 46.

Froomkin, A. M. (2000). The Death of Privacy? *Stanford Law Review* 52(5), p. 1461.

Ness, E. (1994). Big Brother at Cyberspace: Will Your Freedom and Privacy Be Roadkill on the Information Superhighway? *The Progressive* (December), pp. 22-27.

Encryption

While the use of coded messages is nothing new, the Internet and e-commerce have made encryption an important issue in our everyday lives as we send personal information, in some cases, around the world. Most computer systems use one of two types of encryption: public key or symmetric key. Public-key encryption utilizes a combination of a private and a public key. For example, a local computer may hold the private key and give the public key to any other computer that wants to communicate with it. In order to decode a message, a computer must use the public key and its own private key. One example of this is the Transport Layer Security protocol used in webservers. Most browsers have a TLS indicator at the bottom of the browser window; usually a lock icon—look for it the next time you surf the Web. Microsoft offers 128-bit encryption in Internet Explorer, which is the highest level the company can legally allow. In fact, some countries are not allowed to communicate with the U.S. with high-level encryption. In symmetric-key encryption, each computer has its own key (or code) that it can use to encipher an information packet prior to sending it over a network. This type requires that the communicating computers know each other and know the same code; any other computer sees the message as garbage.

BIBLIOGRAPHY

Tyson, J. How encryption works. Howstuffworks.com. Available at http://computer.howstuffworks.com/encryption.htm. Accessed September 21, 2005.

E-Waste

There is no doubt that Americans love computers and electronic gadgets and gizmos. Cell phones, iPods, BlackBerrys, cameras, big screens, little screens, games, and all the other devices that provide entertainment, connectivity, and work-related capabilities are part of almost everybody's life. A common joke is that as soon as a product hits the shelves, it is outdated. New and better versions are always waiting in the wings. Whether this is planned obsolescence or just normal development might be open to debate, but the fact remains that many people are constantly updating and acquiring new electronic devices. What happens to the items that are cast aside in favor of the latest and greatest? Too often the answer is that they are simply discarded, joining other rejects to result in the growing problem of electronic or e-waste.

E-waste is accumulating at a rate triple that of ordinary household trash, and a large amount of it is finding its way into landfills. There the components in discarded equipment are posing a growing problem because they contain a frightening array of toxic materials, such as lead, zinc, copper, antimony, chromium, and tin. These potentially dangerous elements can then leach into soil and water, causing problems yet to be evaluated or addressed. If devices are burned, they emit noxious fumes, further causing environmental woes. Exposure to these elements can cause health risks to both children and adults. Developmental problems may be a side effect in the young, while adults may be affected by endocrine problems, respiratory ailments, and other health issues. One example of the magnitude of the problem has been cited by Elizabeth Royte (2005), author of *Garbage Land,* who reports that tens of millions of cell phones end up in landfills each year. Given the plethora of gadgets appearing almost daily in our society, this trend can only be expected to increase. Ironically, other parts of the world, such as Africa and Asia, are busily destroying ecosystems to mine many of these same elements to further fuel our hunger for all things electronic.

Ideally, all outdated equipment would be refurbished or recycled, but it is not as easy as it sounds. Recycling is expensive, dangerous, and labor intensive, says Royte (2005). Many computer and electronics manufacturers oppose mandated recycling for fear that it will drive up their costs if they are asked, as some states have done, to provide responsible means for discarding their products. Certainly there are initiatives that do just that, including the practice in many businesses of donating replaced computers to schools and charities. One interesting example of a commercial entity addressing the problem is eBay's Rethink Initiative, which directs users to nearby recyclers and provides a program for erasing hard drives to encourage people to responsibly discard computers. Action has also been demonstrated by a growing number of state governmental agencies, such as a bans on e-waste in landfills coupled with the encouragement of recycling. Concern has reached the national level as well, where a congressional

Components in discarded equipment are posing a growing problem because they contain a frightening array of toxic materials, such as lead, zinc, copper, antimony, chromium, and tin. These potentially dangerous elements can then leach into soil and water, causing problems yet to be evaluated or addressed. (*Source:* © iStockphoto.com/VanDusen, Jessica, "Trashed TV." Available at http://www.istockphoto.com.)

working group was formed in 2005 to study standardizing state regulations regarding e-waste (Saying "So Long" to E-waste, 2005). Clearly e-waste is a problem that calls out for attention and awareness on the part of the general public as well as manufacturers and governmental concerns, before it reaches insurmountable proportions.

BIBLIOGRAPHY

Royte, E. (2005). E-Gad! *Smithsonian* 36 (August), pp. 82-87.
Saying "So Long" to E-Waste. (2005). *Christian Science Monitor* 97(August 8), p. 8.
Ursery, S. (2005). EBay Fights E-Waste. *Waste Age* 36 (February), pp. 6-8.

File Swapping

In the early 1980s swapping computer files consisted of small groups of colleagues in computer/math classrooms literally swapping 5 ¼" floppy disks or copying the disks themselves. By the end of any academic year, maybe ten people had questionable copies of *Lemonade Stand* or *The Oregon Trail*; at least these were educational games. Every once in a while someone would have *Swashbuckler* or *Choplifter.* Music swapping also took place. Some music listeners had a high-speed dual cassette deck that would allow the copying of cassette tapes in about two minutes. A TDK SA-90 audio tape could hold two albums, front and back. Others would borrow the really big top-loading VCRs and record movies from HBO or another VCR. The movies looked horrible and usually sounded even worse, but at least users could add them to their library.

Jump forward twenty years. Media swapping and copying has continued. The issue that the software industry, the music industry, and Hollywood have now is that file-swapping software such as Napster, Kazaa, and the like allow file swapping to happen on an international level with millions of people involved.

File swapping itself is an excellent technology. It opens a wide range of collaborative capabilities with individuals worldwide—what the Internet itself did nationally before it became commercialized. File-swapping software allows individuals to upload files to remote servers, while giving search access to files others have posted. The difficulty is that people have been posting copyrighted materials to the servers, everything from software to books and music to movies. Corporations are concerned with losing millions to billions of dollars in sales because of file sharing. The Supreme Court has ruled that file-sharing companies, such as Grokster, could be held liable for copyright piracy on their networks. Justice David Souter wrote in the majority opinion: "We hold that one who distributes a device with the object of promoting its use to infringe copyright, as shown by clear expression or other affirmative steps taken to foster infringement, is liable for the resulting acts of infringement" (*MGM v. Grokster*, 2005, p. 6).

BIBLIOGRAPHY

Borland, J. Supreme Court Rules Against File Swapping. CNetNews.com. Available at http://news.com.com/Supreme+Court+rules+against+file+swapping/ 2100-1030_3-5764135.html. Accessed September 21, 2005.

Metro-Goldwyn-Mayer v. Grokster, Ltd., 545 U.S.___ (2005). Available at http://www.supremecourtus.gov/opinions/04pdf/04-480.pdf. Accessed July 28, 2006.

Firewall

A firewall is a hardware, software, or combination security solution that examines each digital packet of information entering or leaving a network and authorizes or denies passage. In addition to hardware and software firewalls, some operating systems such as Windows XP, when updated with Service Pack 2, provide firewall capability. Operating system firewalls are generally not regarded to be as secure as those created by hardware or independent software. The presence of a firewall is important in preventing unauthorized entry to networked computers.

One issue that affects the need for a firewall involves how the network deals with Internet Protocol addressing. An Internet protocol (IP) address is a number that identifies a computer workstation to all other computers on the Internet. Networked computers with Internet access have two options for having an IP address assigned. The computer may have an IP address dynamically assigned from a batch of IP addresses available on a network server. With the dynamic setup, the computer is assigned a different IP each time a user accesses the Internet. The other option involves having a static number assigned. With the static IP assignment, the computer always keeps the same IP number each time a user from that computer accesses the Internet.

Without a firewall, computers with static IP addresses are more vulnerable from outside attack because any time the computer is on, an unauthorized user who knows the static number may gain access. With a firewall in place entry would likely be denied.

Firewalls have several configuration options that define how restrictive the firewall is in terms of allowing information exchange. For example schools or businesses may use configuration options that restrict access to the network from outside while allowing employee, student, or teacher users to download information, programs, or java scripts from specific Web sites.

BIBLIOGRAPHY

Amberg, E. (2000). Software Focus on Security. *T H E Journal* 27(11), p. 98.

Weafer, V. (2002). Blended Threats: A Deadly Duo of Hackers and Mobile Code. *T H E Journal* 30(5), pp. 16-21.

Flame Wars

Nothing brings out the worst in people like an angry flame war. Hurling insults is a time-honored tradition that long ago inspired eloquence on the part of Shakespeare and of course was popular far before his time. On the Internet, verbal attacks become silent but just as poisonous, often occurring on message boards and in Usenet groups. Freed from the constraints of face-to-face interaction in which people can add body language, facial expression, and voice tone to their understanding of what is said, Internet conversation relies only on what is written. Thus there is greater likelihood that someone may misread a comment and take offense. According to Webopedia.com, a flame is "a searing e-mail or newsgroup message in which the writer attacks another participant in overly harsh, and often personal, terms." Flame wars are angry exchanges between participants, particularly prevalent in forums in which there is no monitor to police people's communications. A flame war can start from almost anything, and sometimes takes the original communicator by surprise. It may begin when someone innocently posts an idea, opinion, or even question to a group. Someone else takes offense and fires back an angry response. The originator retaliates in kind and other people join in. The tenor and language escalate to all-out hostility, replete with insults and profanity. Sometimes people like to start altercations just for fun. Such a troublemaker might intentionally throw out a "flame bait" message on a topic sure to rile people up, such as politics or religion. Again the result is a flurry of exchanges ranging from sarcastic to condescending to downright scary. When the message group is set up so that members can retain anonymity, using only assumed names, there is a greater chance for flame wars to erupt. Such an environment allows people to separate themselves from their words and the consequences of what they say. Messages posted in anger are often fired off without consideration to fact or thought about the results of what is said. Reason and moderation go out the window as the argument escalates. In today's society where people are often polarized in their views and yet likely to meet up online with more people who hold opposing views, it is no wonder that flame wars thrive. Although most such altercations are relatively harmless, in rare cases they lead to cyber stalking and other threatening behavior. The best course in a situation in which a flame war appears to be going too far is to walk away and let the other person have the last word. Continuing will not bring about a peaceful conclusion, and is likely a waste of time and peace of mind.

BIBLIOGRAPHY

Goldsborough, R. and Page, L. (2005). How to Respond to Flames (Without Getting Singed). *Information Today* 22 (February), pp. 23-24.

Webopedia.com. Flame. Available at http://www.webopedia.com. Accessed July 16, 2006.

Flash Mobs

Remember happenings? If so you remember the 1960s. Happenings or "be-ins" were preplanned events where people would show up in public places and carry out scripted actions. They started out as performance art events, but became less "arty" as the craze spread.

Today's answer to "happenings" is the flash mob. Participants show up in response to e-mail and cell phone summonings, converge upon a predetermined location, and briefly and in unison perform some unexplained act, then quickly disperse. According to Schnayerson (2003), one example involved a large group of people who gathered in New York's Central Park, called out the words "nature, nature," chirped like birds, and then left. The fad cropped up in 2003 and became popular around the globe. Supposedly the first incident occurred in a London furniture store, although New Yorkers also claim to have had the first flash mob.

Interestingly the term was adapted for a more constructive purpose by computer science students at the University of San Francisco. Their idea was to gather 1,000 laptop computer users, have them run software designed to maximize their speed, and merge their computations over a single local area network. The result would be an "ad hoc supercomputer" that could run faster than existing supercomputers and possibly give rise to a new type of computer use (Quick as a Flash, 2004).

As with happenings, flash mobs have no particular redeeming value other than to relieve boredom and give people something to talk about. At worst they may cause some people inconvenience; at best they are entertaining. Again, as with happenings, flash mobs will likely have a short life as a popular fad, fading away as the novelty wears off.

BIBLIOGRAPHY

Quick as a Flash. (2004). *New Scientist* (April 14), 182, p. 6.
Shnayerson, Maggie (2003). Flash Mobs. *Time* 162 (August 18), p. 29.

Google Bombing

Google bombing is a type of mischief practiced by pranksters who take advantage of a loophole in the search engine Google's algorithms. A given site will be promoted in rankings if a number of other sites with a key phrase are linked to it (Tatum, 2005). Thus, if a group of people use the phrase "worthless fool" in their Web sites, and link to another Web page, the targeted site will come up in a search for that phrase. As John Hiler (2002) puts it, "the *linker* can impact the Google Rank of the *linkee*." According to Hiler, this technique was first used by Adam Mathes, who played a trick on his friend Andy Pressman so that when "talentless hack" was typed into Google, Andy's Web site became the number one result for the search.

This joke inspired foes of George W. Bush, who used the tactic to cause the president's official biography to come up first in a Google search for the phrase "miserable failure." The fact that Google bombing can be used as a political statement inspired Clifford Tatum (2005) to assert that it is a form of social movement. To support his claims, he described the Bush situation and also an instance in which people displaced an anti-Semitic page by bombing to elevate another page defining the word "Jew." However, while a group effort can definitely change a page's ranking, Google does move most Google bomb links to archive pages after several weeks, thus defusing the bombs.

BIBLIOGRAPHY

Hiler, J. (2002) Google Time Bomb: Will Weblogs Blow Up the World's Favorite Search Engine? (March 3). Available at http://www.microcontentnews.com/articles/googlebombs.htm. Accessed July 16, 2006.

Tatum, C. (2005). Deconstructing Google Bombs: A Breach of Symbolic Power or Just a Goofy Prank? (October). Available at http://www.firstmonday.org. Accessed July 16, 2006.

Cybersins and Digital Good Deeds
© 2007 by The Haworth Press, Inc. All rights reserved.
doi:10.1300/5632_07

71

Google Book Search

Google is the search tool everyone knows and loves. The brainchild of two Stanford graduate students who decided to combine talents in 1996 to improve Internet searching, Google has grown to immense popularity. Indeed the name has been morphed into a verb, as in "I googled that topic and found tons of information." People love the clean, uncluttered lines of the Google main search page and the clever adaptations for special occasions and holidays. Not an entity to sit on its laurels, Google is constantly increasing its fan base with attractive additional features. Google Image Search is so ubiquitous that many people fail to recognize that the pictures do not "come from Google" but rather from the original sites that Google serves up to them. Other features such as Google Desktop Search and Google Scholar offer more specialized services, which are eagerly adopted by those who find them useful.

In December 2004 Google rolled out its most daring and controversial new option, Google Book Search (previously known as Google Print). According to Wiggins et al. (2005) the announcement that Google will digitally scan collections from selected major libraries, including Harvard, University of Michigan, Stanford, Oxford University, and the New York Public Library, brought equal parts dismay and rejoicing. The issues that caused dismay were copyright and the future of traditional libraries. Although the New York Public Library allowed scans of rare and public domain books only, Stanford and Michigan consented to the scanning of their entire collections. The scanning is to be conducted on site and each library will receive a copy of the results with a second copy to be held by Google.

The first burning question is what will Google do with these scanned volumes? The plan is to make from them a searchable database whereby the user can conduct an inquiry and learn what books offer pertinent information. He or she can then seek to obtain the books, with library holdings in his or her area that have the volume provided along with search results. Google insists it does not intend to make the books available online full text, but rather to use the scanned information to help people find books for checkout or purchase, thus increasing open access to information for all users.

The announcement of the Google Book Search project was met with an outcry of protest, especially from publishers who insist that copyright is being violated by the scanning of any works not in public domain (Flagg, 2005). Google responded that, since it was not publishing the text of books but merely reporting their whereabouts, the practice is entirely within the limits of copyright law. Reactions from authors, librarians, and the general public are mixed. Some say that Google Book Search only increases access to information and may actually increase book sales, while others side with the publishers and state books should not be scanned without author/publisher permissions.

An interesting side issue regarding Google Book Search is the secrecy surrounding the whole project. Google refuses to share information about exactly how the books are being scanned. Do humans turn the pages so a device can scan them, or is the action executed robotically? Google will not say. What were the terms of the agreements with the universities? Google again will not talk, and even the joining universities do not know the terms agreed upon by their co-participants. Rumor has it that some schools got "better deals" than others, thus increasing the aura of mystery surrounding the project.

To date, no court rulings have been handed down affecting Google Book Search and many watchers are adopting a wait-and-see attitude about the project and its potential success or failure. Everyone agrees that it is a daring step that was inevitable at some point since the technology is clearly available to make the scanning economically feasible. In all likelihood, Google Book Search will be remembered as an early foray into the new world of libraries, publishing, and information access.

BIBLIOGRAPHY

Flagg, G. (2005). Publishers Question Google Print Library Project. *American Libraries* 36 (August), pp. 15-16.

Wiggins, R., Tennant, R., and Smith, A. (2005). Google Print (conference presentation). Internet Librarian West 2005, Monterey, CA. (October 26).

Google Stalking

Ever want to find someone whom you have not seen in a while? Wonder whatever happened to the girlfriend in high school? Most people think about these kind of things. Web users are using search engines to find the answers to these questions, just by typing in a name. Narcissists might also use this technique to find out information about themselves—mostly what they, themselves, might have published. For example, if someone were to type "James L Van Roekel" in the Google search, he or she would find several pages about James; work information, vita, publications lists, telephone number, and the like. Pretty cool if James wants to be found by an old friend. Or is it really James? Because he has a not very common name, it may be easier to find information on him than John Smith. If someone were to Google search "Mary Ann Bell," the first hit could be a recipe for Mary Ann's Bell Peppers. On the whole, pretty accurate, pretty harmless; or is it?

Cyberstalking is an extension of the physical form of stalking, in which computers and the Internet are used to pursue, harass, or contact another person in an unsolicited fashion. Because of the nature of the Internet, criminals maintain relative anonymity across the globe using the same networks that we use for browsing libraries, ordering tools, accessing our bank statements, and reading the news. Individuals may seek out and harass others through a wide variety of means, including the Web, and this may present a range of physical, emotional, and psychological consequences to the victim.

What can be done about the negative use of personal information? According to Danny Sullivan, editor of SearchEngineWatch.com, "If you don't want people to know about your personal details, don't put them out on the web in any way, shape or form. People say they can't believe their resume is online, but they put it up on their homepage" (Reuters, 2003).

BIBLIOGRAPHY

Google Stalking—A Beginner's Guide. Available at http://technology.nzoom.com/cda/printable/1,1856,175193,00.html. Accessed February 21, 2005.

Petherick, W. Cyber-stalking: Obsessional Pursuit and the Digital Criminal. Avalable at http://www.crimelibrary.com. Accessed February 15, 2005.

Reuters (2003). Stalkers, the Merely Curious Troll for Lost Acquaintances Online. *USA Today* (March 12). Available at http://www.usatoday.com/tech/webguide/internetlife/2003-03-12-net-search_x.htm. Accessed July 28, 2006.

GPS and Privacy

Anyone who watches network television knows a little about GPS, or global positioning systems. Commercials show people who are lost, hurt in accidents, or are victims of crime but are saved by their wonderful automobile tracking systems. Crime shows feature plots in which the bad guy is nailed because he could be similarly hunted down. Although this is not quite as well known, rental agencies often equip their cars with GPS in case they go astray. Outdoors enthusiasts seek out GPS devices as a fail safe against getting lost in the wilderness. It is undeniable that GPS offers the security of knowing that one's whereabouts are never a secret.

One reason people want GPS is to alleviate anxiety. Hikers and their families will not have to worry about them getting lost, and parents of teenagers can have a powerful tool for monitoring their offspring. Anyone with a GPS-equipped car can have the secure feeling that he or she can call for help when something goes wrong. A possible next step might be keeping up with friends. Much like people do with cell phones, individuals could willingly agree to be "buddies" with other GPS users so they could hook up at any given time. Such uses are predicated on the fact that the users (except maybe the teenagers) willingly enter into the agreements to be tracked.

Some people are concerned about the issue of government or law enforcement agencies tracking cell phone users' whereabouts without their knowledge. According to Declan McCullagh (2006), the FBI has been secretly conducting cell phone surveillance in recent years. The authority under which this tracking has been conducted was attributed to the Communications Assistance for Law Enforcement Act of 1994, despite the fact that at the time Director Louis Freeh pledged it would not be used for this purpose. It is likely that few people want to forbid the use of cell phone tracking with due cause in the case of criminal activity. However, the thought that it could happen without adequate safeguards is worrisome and should be addressed. Currently, court hearings have produced mixed results. A January 2006 ruling in Wisconsin found the surveillance unlawful, but shortly thereafter a Louisiana court upheld the practice. Until the matter is settled, it is likely that the surveillance and subsequent controversy will continue (McCullagh, 2006).

Privacy experts point to other troubling issues related with GPS. Tracking systems are growing in popularity as means of following work vehicles. Thus people whose jobs involve driving could be followed throughout their workdays. Such systems are presently in use and can monitor driving speeds, braking, sharp turns and other safety issues as well as a vehicle's whereabouts.

Add such capabilities to the fact that by the end of 2005 all new cell phones were required to have GPS, and we approach a society where it is very hard to move about without someone knowing our whereabouts. As with biometrics, this leads to the possibility of misuse by individuals or agencies exerting too much control over our movements, or tracking us down for less than beneficial purposes. As with many technologies, GPS is a double-edged sword and users need to be aware of the concerns as well as the benefits.

BIBLIOGRAPHY

Levy, S. (2004). A Future With Nowhere to Hide? *Newsweek* 23 (June 7), p. 76.

McCullagh, D. (2006). Perspective: E-Tracking Through Your Cell Phone. CNET News (February 13). Available at http://www.cnet.com. Accessed July 19, 2006.

Waxer, C. (2005). Navigating Privacy Concerns to Equip Workers With GPS. *Workforce Management* 84 (August), pp. 71-73.

Hackers, Crackers, and Hacking

The term *hacker* has come to refer to anyone who is skilled with computers, computer systems, and networks. The term is also used to identify those who are able to gain unauthorized access to computers. Hacking that involves unauthorized access is an illegal activity and could result in criminal charges being filed.

Although the terms *hacker* or *hacking* have been used in reference to those who gain illegal computer access, the term *cracker* (one who cracks a computer, network, or security system) is also used. The hacker or cracker is able to bypass security systems, such as firewalls, and gain unauthorized access to files.

Hackers have been known to access military and financial records. Prison terms have been given to the more high-profile violators who have stolen large sums from their online victims.

Schools have not been immune. The mischief done by hackers in schools often involves an array of offenses such as changing grades, accessing school financial files and gaining access to teacher test banks. Because some students are proficient as hackers or crackers, school networks need the security of a firewall system powerful enough to protect files stored on school servers and on teachers' computers.

In addition to adding a firewall to a network, one other strategy that has been particularly helpful in dealing with hackers is to employ skilled hackers to make recommendations about how to make a network safer.

BIBLIOGRAPHY

Hatcher, M., McDannel, J. and Ostfeld, S. (1999). Computer Crimes. *American Criminal Law Review* 36(3), p. 397.

Cybersins and Digital Good Deeds
© 2007 by The Haworth Press, Inc. All rights reserved.
doi:10.1300/5632_08

Seper, J. (2000). "Suspect, 15 Arrested in Internet Hacking." *The Washington Times* (April 20), p. 1.

Wible, B. (2003). A Site Where Hackers Are Welcome: Using Hack-In Contests to Shape Preferences and Deter Computer Crime. *Yale Law Journal* 112(6), pp. 1577-1624.

Hacktivism

Hacktivism is the melding of two activities mentioned elsewhere in this book, hacking and activism/political protests. The term was coined to describe online organized attacks against companies or organizations that protesters want to damage or disrupt. One goal of "hactivists" is to bypass censors in countries where free speech is inhibited. Users of specialized software can access small, private networks and exchange encrypted files. This tactic is being employed in China and other countries with restrictive and authoritarian leadership. Hacktivismo (www.hacktivismo.com) is an international organization point for protesters worldwide who want to learn about protesting in this manner.

Some actions of hactivists are more disruptive. They include distributed denial of service (DDS) attacks against corporations whose polices they do not like. Enabled by specialized software, DDS attacks have successfully halted operations at both Yahoo and eBay. Politics are often the reason for hactivism. Attacks have been made on the World Trade Organization by those who oppose globalization, on the Mexican government by Zapatistas, and numerous other targets.

As activist hackers gain sophisticated techniques for interrupting services, companies and educational and governmental agencies fight back with increased security measures. Most hactivists use more than one Web-hosting facility to make it harder to bring them down. This push and shove is bound to continue.

BIBLIOGRAPHY

Clark, E. (2000). Flower Power Cyber Style. *Network Magazine* 15 (May), p. 20.
Hacktivismo. Available at http://www.hactivismo.com. Accessed July 16, 2006.

Hoaxes

Internet hoaxes are typically promulgated by chain e-mail with messages about free money, politics, and all other imaginable issues. We all receive these almost daily. Part of the problem is that readers are asked to send these e-mails to everyone they know. Hoaxbusters, an urban legend Web site, describes how to recognize a hoax or chain letter: first, there is a hook, to catch interest and get the reader to read the letter. Common hooks include such provacative message titles as "Free Money!," "Danger!," "Virus Alert," or "A Little Girl Is Dying," which tie into users' fear for the survival of their computers or into sympathy for some poor unfortunate soul. Next comes the threat. Most threats play on greed or sympathy to get the letter passed on. The threat often contains official- or technical-sounding language that enhances its believability. The e-mails often admonish the reader to "distribute this letter to as many people as possible."

One of my favorite hoaxes was a recent e-mail I received from a family member. It is about a great view of the planet Mars:

> The Red Planet is about to be spectacular! This month and next, Earth is catching up with Mars in an encounter that will culminate in the closest approach between the two planets in recorded history. The next time Mars may come this close is in 2287. Due to the way Jupiter's gravity tugs on Mars and perturbs its orbit, astronomers can only be certain that Mars has not come this close to Earth in the Last 5,000 years, but it may be as long as 60,000 years before it happens again. The encounter will culminate on August 27th when Mars comes to within 34,649,589 miles of Earth and will be (next to the moon) the brightest object in the night sky. It will attain a magnitude of -2.9 and will appear 25.11 arc seconds wide. At a modest 75-power magnification Mars will look as large as the full moon to the naked eye. Mars will be easy to spot. At the beginning of August it will rise in the east at 10 p.m. and reach its azimuth at about 3 a.m. By the end of August when the two planets are closest, Mars will rise at nightfall and reach its highest point in the sky at 12:30 a.m. That's pretty convenient to see something that no human being

has seen in recorded history. So, mark your calendar at the beginning of August to see Mars grow progressively brighter and brighter throughout the month. Share this with your children and grandchildren. NO ONE ALIVE TODAY WILL EVER SEE THIS AGAIN!

Although much of the information in this message is true, uninformed sky watchers will surely be disappointed since the event had taken place in 2003.

BIBLIOGRAPHY

Hoaxbusters. CIAX Internet Hoax Information. Available at http://hoaxbusters.ciac .org/HBHackedHistory.shtml#mars. Accessed September 20, 2005.

Identity Theft and the Internet

Identity theft using the Internet involves the assumption of another person's identity often for the purpose of creating new fraudulent accounts, gaining access to the victim's existing accounts, or establishing credentials that allow the criminal to use the name of the victim for illegal or questionable purposes. Identity theft has become a significant problem in our country, causing in some cases substantial financial and personal woes for its victims. Victims not only suffer potential economic loss but also suffer from the loss of their good name as they try to reestablish credit and to convince others that they are innocent of creating a new account filled with illegal charges or of withdrawing funds from an existing account.

Criminals develop both simple and elaborate schemes to gather information that would allow them to assume another's identity. Potential victims may counter the efforts of the criminals by adopting some commonsense practices aimed at ensuring that personal information does not fall into the wrong hands. A few of those practices include:

- Getting regular copies of credit reports and noting any new inexplicable account or activity.
- Using common sense in developing passwords for accounts. If a criminal has researched facts about a person, that criminal may know a social security number or a mother's maiden name. Develop passwords that do not come from past history.
- Shredding all unsolicited mail. Credit card solicitors often require a minimal amount of information to create an account.
- Checking bank statements for errors.
- Carrying mail to the post office. Don't leave it in an unprotected mailbox.
- Being cautious about ordering information over wireless networks. Small wireless routers allow access 150 feet or more from the base, and neighbors can access a network from a nearby house.

Cybersins and Digital Good Deeds
© 2007 by The Haworth Press, Inc. All rights reserved.
doi:10.1300/5632_09

Identity theft allows a person to access legitimate accounts or create fraudulent new ones.

Identity theft can go beyond monetary theft. Information gained improperly may also be used by terrorists for obtaining passports and for international travel.

BIBLIOGRAPHY

Bielski, L. (2001). Identity Theft. *ABA Banking Journal* 93(1), p. 27.

Castiglione, N. D. (2002). "My Social Security Number Is": Some Common Sense Ways to Fight Identity Theft. *ABA Banking Journal* 94(12), pp. 57-59.

Identity Theft Fastest Growing White Collar Crime in Nation. (2003). *State Legislatures* (April), p. 9.

Milne, G. R. (2003). How Well Do Consumers Protect Themselves from Identity Theft? *Journal of Consumer Affairs* 37(2), pp. 388-402.

Internet Pornography

According to Internet Filter Review (2002), Internet pornography accounted for 2.5 percent or $2.5 billion of the $57 billion made in the pornography industry. Internet pornography sites make up approximately 12 percent of all Web sites, with 4.2 million sites and 372 million pages. No one doubts how easy it is to get to pornography sites on the Internet. A Google search of any sex- or pornography-related term results in hundreds of hits, including advertising. Because of the ease of access to these sites, many public libraries and corporations utilize filtering software that blocks these sites from view of the institution's computers. In December 2000, Congress passed the Children's Internet Protection Act, mandating filters in all schools and libraries that receive federal financial assistance through the E-rate or Universal Service Fund program, or through the Library Services and Technology Act. This amounts to about 60 percent of the nation's libraries and public schools.

Some difficulty has been experienced with these filters. In fact, on September 11, 2005, Websense categorized technology writer John Dvorak's Web site as a sex site: "My numbers tumbled today and I've been getting email from people at the USDA and elsewhere saying the site has been categorized as a sex site despite the incredible lack of sex on the site! Google Adsense would have banned me long before now. I think something is fishy" (Dvorak, 2005).

BIBLIOGRAPHY

Dvorak, J. (2005). Websense Categorized *Dvorak Uncensored* Blog as SEX-Oriented. Site Banned Nationwide by Large Enterprises—Political Motivation Suspected. *Dvorak Uncensored*. Available at http://www.dvorak.org/blog/?p=2780. Accessed July 21, 2006.

Hein, M. and Cho, C. (2001). Internet Filters: A Public Policy Report. *NCAC On the Issues*. National Coalition Against Censorship. Available at http://www.ncac.org/issues/internetfilters.html. Accessed September 20, 2005.

Internet Pornography Statistics. (2002). *Internet Filter Review*. Available at http://internet-filter-review.toptenreviews.com/internet-pornography-statistics.html. Accessed July 21, 2006.

Internet User Agreement and the Library

An Internet User Agreement outlines the conditions under which a computer user may access the Internet in a public facility such as a library. In schools the term *Acceptable Use Policy* identifies similar responsibilities for student Internet users.

Although plans vary, the following represents a list of common Internet User Agreements required of those who wish to access the Internet from a library.

> User agrees to a limited number of hours or minutes of Internet access.
>
> User agrees not to access a site that might be threatening or harassing to library staff or to other users.
>
> User agrees to use only filtered access if the user is under 18.
>
> User understands that information on the Internet is subject to the same standards of academic merit as a printed text and that Internet information may be outdated, inaccurate, or biased.
>
> User agrees not to install or download software.
>
> User agrees to follow copyright laws and software licensing agreements.
>
> User agrees not to participate in commercial activities.
>
> User agrees not to send chain letters or broadcast messaging.
>
> User understands that he/she is not to engage in any criminal activity on the Internet.
>
> User agrees to limit the number of pages printed.
>
> User agrees not to access information that could reasonably be judged as pornography.
>
> User understands that the library retains the right to monitor Internet use.
>
> User agrees not to transmit information with known viruses, worms or Trojan horses.
>
> User agrees to library restrictions concerning the use of e-mail and chat rooms.

User agrees not to hack into other computers.
User agrees to library restricts on FTP transmissions.

Enforcement of an Internet User Agreement in a public library usually falls to the librarian. The librarian's choice of actions to take for those who violate the agreement may vary from limiting library resources to notifying law enforcement officials for more serious offenses.

BIBLIOGRAPHY

Dyrli, O. E. (2000). Is Your Acceptable Use Policy Acceptable? *Curriculum Administrator* (September), p. 29.

Marker, G. (1996). Social Studies and the Internet: Developing a School Policy. *Social Studies* 87(6), pp. 244-248.

Sanchez, R. (1996). Students on the Internet: Can You Ensure Appropriate Access? *School Administrator* (April), p. 18.

Keystroke Logging

As with many other devices or programs, keystroke loggers were designed with a constructive intent but have also been used for nefarious practices. A key logger can be a small device that is attached physically to a computer or, more likely, a small program downloaded to a hard drive. If the key logger is a hardware peripheral, it will appear as a small object placed between the CPU and the keyboard cable plug. To the uninitiated, it would likely go unnoticed, especially since most jacks for keyboards are on the backs of computers. If a program is used, it may well be installed without user knowledge as part of a spyware or Trojan horse invasion. Once the key logger is installed, it lives up to its name by recording every keystroke typed by users of that particular computer.

Why would someone want to save and peruse all keystrokes? Parents and suspicious spouses may purchase key logging devices to keep up with the communications and activities of their children or partners. Businesses may monitor employees' work-time computer usage. Of course the flip side of such practices is the inevitable invasion of privacy. According to Donna Edwards (2004) one example from the business world is the case that resulted in the first federal wiretapping prosecution involving the use of a key logging device. In this instance, an individual was trying to access a co-worker's client database and use it for his own profit.

One of the greatest misuses of key loggers is accessing other people's passwords, says Andrew Brandt (2004). In Texas an enterprising student attached a device to his teacher's computer, obtained passwords, and then removed the device. He thus gained access to student records, including grades, and caused considerable damage. People have had account information and financial records accessed by key loggers who steal passwords. Of course such invasions are against the law, but they are hard to catch and trace, especially since users are often unaware that anything is amiss. Indeed some experts

Cybersins and Digital Good Deeds
© 2007 by The Haworth Press, Inc. All rights reserved.
doi:10.1300/5632_10

are predicting the end of the "age of the password" because of com-promises by key loggers. Some businesses are presently moving to dual passwords, one supplied by the user and another by the supervis-ing agency. At the same time, security experts are working to come up with alternatives to passwords, which are increasingly considered outdated and inadequate forms of protecting users and data.

How can the average user protect against invasion by key loggers? A physical device is easy to spot once a user knows to look for one. To avoid the software version, the careful user should be sure to use anti-spyware as well as virus protection. Also, one should be careful about downloading from the Internet and avoid temptation to download from questionable sites.

BIBLIOGRAPHY

Brandt, A. (2004). Two Passwords Double Your Privacy. *PC World* 22 (Septem-ber), p. 46.

Edwards, D. (2004). Talking Tech: Free Software Just May Be Spying On You! (April 13). Available at http://www.richmond.com. Accessed July 16, 2006.

Whatis?com. Keylogger. Available at http://whatis.techtarget.com. Accessed July 16, 2006.

Logging On As an Administrator

When a computer user logs into a workstation connected to other workstations and/or to a server on the network, he or she gains access to files, programs, and services as defined by a network administrator. The privileges available to the user are defined either through rights associated with each user name or through a profile of common users.

The privileges available to the user at log-in are linked with the name and password entered as he or she begins using the workstation. A user who improperly gains access to the user name and password of the network administrator and enters that information on a workstation at the time of log-in would be given privileges allowing the user to play havoc with either that individual workstation, with the server,

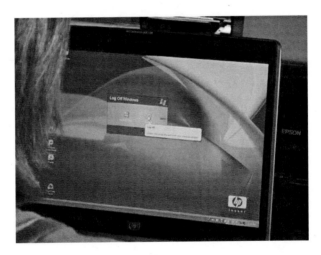

Network systems operators must be careful to log off after using a workstation or server. If they do not, the next user may access the network with a systems operator's privileges.

and/or with the whole operation of the network. Changes that could be made by an unauthorized user might include changing the settings on individual workstations, installing software, accessing and changing server configurations, and changing user or profile privileges.

The potential problems that might occur call to mind some common-sense precautions that all workstation users and network administrators should follow. The first precaution is for all users and administrators to log off after using a computer workstation. Failing to log off could potentially allow another user to approach the machine and access files based upon the privileges defined for the previous user. In addition, network administrators should take special precautions with their user names and passwords to ensure that others do not gain access to that information.

BIBLIOGRAPHY

Amberg, E. (2000). Software Focus on Security. *T H E Journal* 27(11), p. 98.

Logo Abuse

In a world that increasingly relies upon visual designs to identify meaning, more and more thought is going into the type of designs that represent a commercial product or service. Those who create the designs search for a unique expression that captures in an imaginative way the essence of a product or service.

The design itself may be text, a graphical symbol or a combination of the two. Popular graphic and text business designs have come to be identified with the word *logo*.

Logos are commonplace today. Everything from athletics teams to restaurants to technology products can be identified with unique logos. The upside-down horseshoe displayed on a football helmet tells the world that they are watching the Indianapolis Colts National Football League team. The golden arches tell a child who can't read that he or she is near McDonald's. A four-color flag tells the user that he or she is working with a Microsoft product.

The effectiveness of the logo as a representative symbol of the company causes a need for protecting its use by unscrupulous users. These users may take a logo and attach it to a different product or service and, in so doing, attempt to convince others that the fake product or service is legitimate. Inferior products from purses to tennis shoes have been stamped with a legitimate logo and sold as an authentic product.

With the advent of the Internet, criminals have developed electronic fraudulent strategies that allow them to take the logo from a legitimate Web site and to add it to a bogus one. Internet users then are encouraged to buy a counterfeit service or product or to provide account information that would allow the criminals to use the information to create new accounts or to access existing ones.

BIBLIOGRAPHY

"Internet Scammers Go 'Phishing'; Steal Personal Information by Imitating Legit Web Sites." (2003). *The Washington Times* (April 22), p. A01.

O'Sullivan, O. (2003) Gone "Phishing": This Was the Summer When Consumers Were Lured to Fake Bank Websites with a View to Defrauding Them. *ABA Banking Journal* 95(11), pp. 7-8.

Marketing to Children

Children have been heavily targeted by marketers, especially since the early days of television. It probably goes without saying that this trend was bound to carry over to the Internet. Online advertisers hawking everything from bank accounts to kid fashion have gone after children in a big way.

People in the ad industry herald advertising to kids as a great way to get the word out about products and services. One example is the Tommy Hilfiger site for kids (www.tommy.com/kids), which won an Exceptional Experience Award in 2004 from Organic, Inc., a global marketing ad advertising company. Here youngsters can play games, including an interactive paper-doll experience in which users dress virtual models in the latest Tommy outfits. An online bank account, such as ones offered at Valley National Bancorp (www.valleynational bank.com) and ING Bank (home.ingdirect.com) can get kids started earlier thinking about spending and saving money. Debit and credit cards for children are in the planning stages. As one executive pointed out, having kid accounts has the additional advantage of drawing in their parents as well (Wolfe, 2004).

Toy companies such as Lego (www.lego.com) and Mattel (www.mattel.com), as one might expect, have a long history of advertising to children. The Lego site sports basketball and hockey games. The idea is to get the kids talking about the games and about the toys as well. Hoping to involve even more kids, Lego plans to make game CDs in the hopes of penetrating homes where computers are not online. Mattel also offers such CD games, including ones starring Barbie.

All these tactics are the results of intense study. A 1999 study by Forrester Research titled "The Net Powered Generation" found that youngsters often stay online longer than adults, are more willing to try different things than their parents, and are more likely to go online from numerous locations. Based on this and other information, brand sites tend to have certain characteristics that have been proven to succeed:

- Sites often create the aura of being a special place or world.
- Games and interactive activities such as coloring books and puzzles are featured.
- Clubs and contests for kids are offered.
- Built-in communication, such as chat and e-mail or e-cards, is popular.

One especially creative site is Neopets (www.neopets.com), where kids play games that expose them to numerous brand-name products. If a player adopts a lovable creature from the imaginary world called Neopia, she or he may have to find a cure when the creature is suddenly affected with Neomites, virtual pests. The player can only buy a cure at the Neopian drug store, but it will cost game points. She or he earn points and save the pet by winning games or finding treasure at the site's virtual McDonald's or General Mills Lucky Charms game, thus exposing the player to a number of products at the site. Online advertisers hope, as do their television counterparts, to build upon "pester power," the effect upon parents which causes adults to buy things their children plead to have. They also hope to increase brand recognition and loyalty.

All of this sounds and looks like great fun to children, but many parents, teachers, and psychologists decry such intensive marketing to kids. Research indicates that very young children do not have the ability to tell the difference between regular television programs and commercials. By the same token they are vulnerable to online marketing. Another concern is the increasingly materialistic attitudes of many children, coupled with a sense of entitlement that they should be able to have the things they see regularly touted to them. Further, childhood obesity is partly attributed to children's sedentary hours spent in front of television and computer screens, all the while being bombarded by messages extolling junk food. Finally, opponents of such advertising say youngsters are targeted by makers of increasingly violent video games.

One age range, eight to twelve, has been labeled the "tween" market by advertisers. This group is increasingly offered sites based on teen and adult entertainment. Research shows that eleven-year-olds

Research indicates that very young children do not have the ability to tell the difference between regular television programs and commercials. (*Source:* © iStockphoto.com/Jacobs, Bonnie. "Laptop Kids 2." Available at http//:www .istockphoto.com.)

no longer consider themselves to be children. The Toy Manufacturers of America recently changed their target group from birth to fourteen, lowering the cutoff age to ten. Tweens are likely to be confronted with ads that can be detrimental to their self-esteem based on the unrealistic body images in ads. Further, marketers such as Calvin Klein and Abercrombie & Fitch are often criticized for sensationalizing adult sexuality along with their "cool" clothes for youngsters in their ads.

Concerned adults can fight back by contacting webmasters or broadcasters with objections and concerns. They should also work with children to make them savvier about online advertising. Rampant ads are just one more reason why parents should monitor children's online activities. Trusting advertisers to adhere to guidelines for marketing to children is not enough for concerned adults who want to protect children from excessive advertising.

BIBLIOGRAPHY

Black, S. (2004). Tommy Kids Web Site Wins Kudos. *Apparel Magazine* 2 (August), pp. 8-10.

Fonda, D. (2004). Pitching It To Kids. *Time* 163 (August), pp. 52-55.

Media Awareness Network. (2005). Available at http//www.media-awareness.ca. Accessed July 17, 2006.

Wolfe, D. (2004). Web Sites for Kids Do Double Marketing Duty. *American Banker* 17 (January 7), pp. 12-15.

Media and Cognitive Development

The study of the impact of media upon cognitive development has primarily focused on the role of television and computers. Because of the passive role of young people watching television and because young viewers often don't understand a plot or any details about a television program, the American Academy of Pediatrics (www.aap.org) recommends that children under the age of two should not watch TV at all.

For children over two, evidence suggests that continued monitoring of television time is in order; however, one program, *Sesame Street,* has proven to have a favorable impact upon viewers ages three and up. Results from longitudinal studies suggest that boys and girls who watch *Sesame Street* possess an enhanced vocabulary and do better academically once those boys and girls begin school. Critics of *Sesame Street* note that the classroom experience may be less appealing than the fast-moving television experience offered on *Sesame Street,* and because of that difference, parents should limit youngsters' time watching the program.

In addition to its impact upon cognitive development, television has demonstrated an impact upon aggressive behaviors in children, a fact that further argues for close television monitoring by parents.

Computers, too, are scrutinized by teachers and parents regarding their impact upon cognitive development. Because computers can require engaging, synthesizing strategies, as well as critical thinking, they receive a more favorable review as instructional tools than does television.

Computers, however, when used instructionally for the purpose of rote or fill-in-the-blank types of activities have little value in developing cognitive skills. Parental supervision and monitoring of computer use by children, like television watching, should be closely enforced.

BIBLIOGRAPHY

Alvermann, D. E. and Hagood, M. C. (2000). Critical Media Literacy: Research, Theory, and Practice in "New Times." *The Journal of Educational Research* 93(3), p. 193.

American Academy of Pediatrics. Available at http://www.aap.org.

Collis, B. A. (1996). *Children and Computers in School.* Mahwah, NJ: Lawrence Erlbaum Associates.

Feldman, R. S. (2003). *Development Across the Life Span.* Upper Saddle River, New Jersey: Pearson, Prentice Hall.

Johnson, M. M. (2001). The Impact of Television and Directions for Controlling What Children View. *Journal of Broadcasting & Electronic Media* 45(4), pp. 680-686.

Osofsky, J. D. (Ed.). (1997). *Children in a Violent Society.* New York: Guilford Press.

Wartella, E. A. and Jennings, N. (2000). Children and Computers: New Technology-Old Concerns. *The Future of Children* 10(2), p. 31.

Modern Luddites

The resurrected term *Luddites* recently reentered our vocabulary and has been applied in the early twenty-first century to those who question the value of digital technology. The term originally was created around 1810 when it was used to identify a movement in northern England in which a group of workers suggested that technology such as the loom undervalued humans and as such should be destroyed. These so-called Luddites, who were named after a possibly mythical leader, Ned Ludd, adopted violent tactics and physically destroyed factories such as cotton mills and related equipment. The movement reached such intensity that it provoked the Frame Breaking Act, a law making the destruction of machinery a capital crime in England. The Luddite movement eventually ended by 1817.

Modern Luddites, on the other hand, focus their criticism mainly on computers and maintain that the use of digital technology impedes real progress. Some modern Luddites argue that technology removes our ability to interact as human beings and thus diminishes a key ingredient of our civilization. Others argue that technology empowers the corporate user at the expense of the individual.

Modern Luddites in the United States have been loosely associated with the Green Party and align themselves with many of the environmental issues supported by the Greens. Different offshoots of the modern Luddites have focused their criticism on the advancement of particular types of technology, such as nanotechnology.

BIBLIOGRAPHY

Brown, A. (2001). Sometimes the Luddites Are Right. *The Futurist* (September), p. 38.

Browne, R. B. and Fishwick, M. W. (Eds.). (1999). *The Global Village: Dead or Alive?* Bowling Green, OH: Bowling Green State University Popular Press.

Haynes, D. J. (1997). On the Need for Ethical Aesthetics: Or, Where I Stand between Neo-Luddites and Cyberians. *Art Journal* 56(3), pp. 75-82.

Tudge, C. (2000). When It's Right to Be a Luddite. *New Statesman* (April 24), p. 25.

Monitoring Employees' Internet Use

Business supervisors are coming to realize that an Internet use policy for employees is needed and that the policy must define legitimate computer use on the job. Several incidents highlight the need. The incidents involve the employee use of computers at work for such non-job-related purposes as participating in chat rooms, using the Internet for accessing personal e-mail, and accessing illegal files. All of these activities impact the productivity of the employee and can, under certain circumstances, lead to litigation against the employer.

Chat rooms may create problems for employers and may under certain circumstances make them liable for employee behavior. One incident involved a male employee who used a company-owned computer to form a relationship in a chat group. The online relationship culminated in a sexual encounter between the user, who was HIV positive, and a female chat user. When the female contacted HIV, she sued her male counterpart's employer suggesting a liability not only for the employee but for the employer as well.

Probably the most frequent use of company computers for non-job-related purposes involves accessing personal e-mail accounts. Many employees consider the practice acceptable; however, both employers and employees concede that the practice impedes worker productivity.

Monitoring employee use of the Internet by employers can cause a backlash. For example, saving illegal files on a company-owned computer obviously falls within the range of unacceptable work behavior; however, the method for accessing the illegal files by the employer has been challenged in court. One incident involved the use of a company-owned computer by an employee who saved child pornography files on his workstation (Muhl, 2003). The files were found by a network administrator, and the administrator took the user's hard drive from the workstation and used the files on the hard drive as evidence against the employee. The employee charged that taking the hard drive was improper in that the Fourth Amendment prevents searches without a warrant. The argument was rejected in court.

The proper use of the Internet at work should be spelled out in an employee Internet use policy. The policy should warn employees that their Internet usage is monitored and remind them that employee files, if requested, may be used in litigation. Policies should also establish that the computer is the property of the company and should be used exclusively for the purposes identified by the company in the policy. Limitations regarding personal e-mail use should also clearly be defined.

Laws have been proposed that specify the conditions for the monitoring of employee computers. The Notice of Electronic Monitoring Act (NEMA) was drafted in 2000. NEMA required that employers notify employees that computer usage was monitored and that the use for information obtained during monitoring must be defined and shared with employees. The proposed act did not pass.

BIBLIOGRAPHY

Burn, T. (1998). "Office E-Mail's Handy, But It Can Get You Fired." *The Washington Times* (April 7), p. 7.

McEvoy, S. A. (2002). E-Mail and Internet Monitoring and the Workplace: Do Employees Have a Right to Privacy? *Communications and the Law* 24(2), p. 69.

Muhl, C. J. (2003). Workplace E-Mail and Internet Use: Employees and Employers Beware: An Employee's Personal Use of an Employer's E-Mail System and of Internet Access Is Not Protected under the Law, and Employers Can Face Legal Liability for Employees' Inappropriate Use Thereof. *Monthly Labor Review* 126(2), pp. 36-45.

Nowak, J. S. (1999). Employer Liability for Employee Online Criminal Acts. *Federal Communications Law Journal* 51(2), p. 467.

Snider, L. (2001). Crimes against Capital: Discovering Theft of Time. *Social Justice* 28(3), pp. 105-120.

Watson, N. (2001). The Private Workplace and the Proposed "Notice of Electronic Monitoring Act": Is "Notice" Enough? *Federal Communications Law Journal* 54(1), pp. 79-102.

Movie Duplication

With the growth of different types of media, the notion of intellectual property has expanded to include an extensive number of media resources, including movies. Movies have been particularly difficult to protect because of their popularity and ease in duplicating.

Those who wish to make copies of movies without regard for the intellectual property rights of their creators do so for a number of reasons. The reasons include making copies to own for personal viewing, to share with others, or to sell for a profit. The methods employed to make the illegal copies include both the use of older as well as more recent technology.

Copying movies from a videocassette recorder (VCR) tape is a technique emanating from the growth of VCR recorders and tapes in the 1980s. Anyone with two recorders could attach video and audio cables between the two and allow one VCR to play a movie while another recorded it. In an attempt to thwart the efforts of movie pirates, distributors placed protections on movie tapes; however, these were not effective in preventing illegal copying.

The advent of the digital age in the 1990s offered a new form for storing movies—the digital video disc (DVD). Copying movies now involved having a computer with at least one DVD player and one DVD writer, although some computers allowed duplication with only a single player/writer. DVD movie producers again used elaborate protections to prevent illegal copies; however, sophisticated software and hardware allowed movie pirates to continue their theft.

Another method for making illegal copies of movies has grown from the capability of digital video cameras that make high-quality images. Movie pirates take these cameras to a movie, sit in the audience, and record the screen. The copy is then duplicated for illegally sharing with others. This method allows an unscrupulous movie attendant to make a copy of a movie during its initial showing. Because of this practice theater supervisors have begun to restrict the use of any type of cameras during the showing of a film.

Illegal duplication of movies impacts movie producers as illegal movie drafts compete with legal copies. The ultimate impact is felt by consumers as ticket prices increase.

BIBLIOGRAPHY

Burton, D. F. (1997). The Brave New Wired World. *Foreign Policy* (Spring), pp. 22-37.

Halbert, D. J. (1999). *Intellectual Property in the Information Age: The Politics of Expanding Ownership Rights.* Westport, CT: Quorum Books.

Marshall, P. (1997). Guarding the Wealth of the Nations. *The Wilson Quarterly* (Winter), pp. 64-70.

No Copying Allowed. (2004). *State Legislatures* (April), p. 11.

Walker, C. R. (1962). *Modern Technology and Civilization: An Introduction to Human Problems in the Machine Age.* New York: McGraw-Hill.

Multimedia Manipulation

A digital image, be it still or moving, is created with the intent of sharing a visual meaning. Similarly, a digital sound byte is created to convey an audio message. These two media resources, digital images and sound segments, may be blended together with the intent of delivering a more powerful meaning or purpose, such as pleasure, instruction, or reflection. To complement the delivery, text may be added to the mix. The capability of using a number of media sources—image, sound, and text—to convey meaning defines a new communication form, multimedia.

More and more of our communications in the twenty-first century involve the creation and mixing of a number of media sources. The advancement of multimedia development has become so important in our society that observers now speculate about the end of text as the primary way information is shared.

Our ability to use and mix a number of digital media sources also gives us the capability to isolate one medium from a multimedia presentation and to manipulate that medium in a way that conveys a quite different meaning. For example, the audio, video, or text used in a television advertisement may be removed and replaced to convey a message not intended by the original creator. A digital presentation of a politician's speech may have the speaker's audio removed and placed with other video, suggesting a quite different meaning than originally intended by the speaker.

Multimedia manipulation has prompted a demand in the academic community for the study of media literacy, a study requiring a critical look at the implications of multimedia development and at the implications of technology capabilities that can isolate and manipulate media resources and can alter meaning in the process.

BIBLIOGRAPHY

Kim, G. H. and Paddon, A. R. (1999). Digital Manipulation as New Form of Evidence of Actual Malice in Libel and False Light Cases. *Communications and the Law* 21(3), p. 57.

Messaris, P. (1994). *Image, Mind, and Reality*. Boulder, CO: Westview Press.

Reinking, D. et al. (Eds.). (1998). *Handbook of Literacy and Technology: Transformations in a Post-Typographic World*. Mahwah, NJ: Lawrence Erlbaum Associates.

Napster

Napster, a Web site and company providing the ability for users to share audio files, took advantage of the networking capability of the Internet by allowing Internet users to obtain music from others without paying for it. The feat was accomplished by converting music to the MP3 format, an audio compression allowing songs to need only a fraction of the storage size normally required by an audio file. The music was then stored on a central server and users could either download musical files to their home computers or upload their own musical files to share.

Napster came into being in June 1999 and was almost immediately under attack by recording artists who complained that Napster was providing a means for people to obtain copies of their music without paying for it. Napster enjoyed enormous popularity until an injunction shut down the company and its Web site in July 2001. In September 2001, Napster agreed to pay $26 million in damages to artists affected by Napster's service. Napster eventually filed for bankruptcy.

The Napster Web site today is owned by Roxio, a company that purchased Napster's resources after the lawsuit. The Napster site currently offers users the opportunity to purchase legal digital copies of any song housed on its server. The success of Napster spawned a number of similar Internet businesses, including iTunes which also allows subscribers to pay for a song and download it legally.

Since developing a legal means to sell and distribute music, Napster has surged in growth. On January 3, 2005, Napster began offering public stock options on Nasdaq under the ticker symbol NAPS.

Cybersins and Digital Good Deeds
© 2007 by The Haworth Press, Inc. All rights reserved.
doi:10.1300/5632_13

The success of the Napster software in allowing the sharing of MP3 files online spawned the creation of a number of companies who today sell music legally to Internet users.

BIBLIOGRAPHY

Burgunder, L. B. (2002). Reflections on Napster: The Ninth Circuit Takes a Walk on the Wild Side. *American Business Law Journal* 39(4), pp. 683-707.

Glanz, W. (2001). Court Rules against Napster. *The Washington Times* (February 13), p. 1.

Greene, S. (2001). Reconciling Napster with the Sony Decision and Recent Amendments to Copyright Law. *American Business Law Journal* 39(1), pp. 57-98.

McKay, J. P. (2002). Life after Napster: New File-Sharing Method Keeps Record Labels Happy. *Black Enterprise* (March), p. 55.

Network Ubiquity

There is no question that the telecommunications industry is growing. How many of us have access to multiple landline telephones, mobile telephones, wireless, wired, cable, DSL, etc., networks? Although remnants of copper wire-based telecommunications networks still exist, fiber is the new standard.

There are typically four classes of optical networks: static networks, wavelength-routed networks, linear lightwave networks, and logically routed networks. These are discussed in increased order of complexity while emphasizing methodologies for network design, control, analysis, and management. Static networks are the simplest form of a transparent optical network and use optical multiplexing and multiple access to provide multipoint connectivity. The most elementary form of this is the broadcast star, in which all signals transmitted are combined at a star coupler and broadcast to all receivers. Wavelength-routed networks use optical switching to provide point-to-point connectivity over reconfigurable optical paths, in which reconfiguration is achieved by space switching. In linear lightwave networks, an optical path consists of a fiber path carried on a designated waveband creating a connection on a designated optical path within the path's waveband to that connection. Logically routed networks use electronically switched overlays to provide virtual connectivity on a reconfigurable optical layer, such as automated teller machine switches or IP routers (Stern, 2002).

Many people use wireless networks, or wi-fi. Read practically any business or computer magazine and you'll find quite a bit of content and advertisements regarding wi-fi. These issues are typically geared to both office-based and home-based users. Mobile computing, paging, e-mail, and telephone services are becoming more prevalent and less expensive in price. Many businesses and restaurants offer free "hotspots" where customers can connect to the Internet with their device while sipping on their double mocha super espresso. This is an interesting dichotomy. Go to the coffee shop to use a wireless hotspot while getting wired on caffeine.

In a wi-fi network, an access point with a small antenna connects computers to the network. This allows for the transmission of data back and forth over radio signals. These signals can travel up to 300 feet indoors. With an outdoor access point the signal can reach out up to thirty miles to serve places such as universities, research facilities, manufacturing plants, industrial locations, golf courses, and the like. The use of these technologies allows access to just about everyone nationwide and, to some, globally.

BIBLIOGRAPHY

Stern, T. E. and Bala, K. (1999). *Multiwavelength Optical Networks: A Layered Approach*. Berkeley, CA: Addison-Wesley.

Van Roekel, J. L. (2002). Review of: Thomas E. Stern and Krishna Bala. (1999). Multiwavelength Optical Networks: A Layered Approach. *Technology Electronic Reviews* 9(3) (July). Available at http://www.lita.org. Accessed July 17, 2006.

$100 MIT Laptop

Announced in January 2005 by MIT Media Lab chair and co-founder Nicholas Negroponte, the $100 laptop is being developed for children around the world in developing economies: "One Laptop per Child." Current specifications include a 500MHz processor, four USB ports, 1GB memory with wireless capabilities that use innovative power—including wind-up (OLPC, 2006).

These machines can be built inexpensively by lowering the cost of the display. The first-generation machine may use a novel, dual-mode LCD display commonly found in inexpensive DVD players, but that can also be used in black and white, in bright sunlight, and at four times the normal resolution—all at a cost of approximately $35. The laptops will be sold in very large numbers (millions) directly to ministries of education, which can distribute them like textbooks. Initial discussions have been held with China, Brazil, Thailand, and Egypt. Additional countries will be selected for beta testing. Initial orders will be limited to a minimum of one million units (with appropriate financing), with preliminary shipments scheduled for late 2006 to early 2007 (OLPC, 2006).

BIBLIOGRAPHY

Negroponte, N. $100 Laptop. *MIT Media Lab*. Available at http://laptop.media.mit.edu. Accessed September 29, 2005.
OLPC. (2006). Frequently Asked Questions. Available at http://www.bptop.org/faq.en_US.html. Accessed July 17, 2006.

doi:10.1300/5632_14

Online Gambling

Many people find relaxation and diversion in gambling. As with other "vices," such as alcohol and tobacco, proponents say that gambling is harmless in moderation. For those who agree, online gambling greatly enhances choices and opportunities to have a little fun. A quick search with any tool will yield countless sites where one can easily log on and begin playing with just a few keystrokes. People who like to wager no longer have to travel to inconvenient locations and have additional costs for commuting, meals, and other expenses. Instead they can stay home and, if they want, participate in several games at once. Those who once might have found it difficult to get out to casinos, racetracks, or other venues because of disability, family obligations, or other impediments can now play from the convenience and comfort of home.

There are, however, a few problems associated with online gambling. For starters, it is illegal in the United States, according to the U.S. Department of Justice (U.S. Shops Must Fold, 2005). Furthermore, the Justice Department warns that it is illegal to "aid and abet" gambling via the Internet by posting ads or transferring money to pay off bets. Many states augment the federal laws with additional measures of their own. These restrictions do not apply elsewhere, and gambling is legalized and controlled in the United Kingdom, Gibraltar, and other locations that offer numerous online sites. Users who participate in such sites as Britain's MoneyGaming.com get around the laws by having funds transferred through third-party entities as opposed to U.S. banks, though eBay's PayPal was recently charged $10 million in fines for violating the Patriot Act by processing transactions (U.S. Shops Must Fold, 2005).

In addition to the murky situation regarding legality of online gambling in the United States, there is the universal problem of gambling as an addiction. People who have a predilection for compulsive gambling no longer have the barriers of time and place, since they can log on anytime and anywhere. In the United Kingdom, this has prompted particular concern regarding women, who previously were less apt to leave home and visit gambling outlets. To combat addictive gambling, online therapy is now being offered by entities such as GamblingTherapy.org.uk.

Online gambling is too popular and profitable to withstand attempts to thwart its use through laws or admonitions. The attraction for people who can gamble responsibly is far too great an opportunity for the gambling industry to resist. Those who are opposed to gambling on moral grounds or because of experiences with the danger of habitual use will need to find ways to deal with the reality of its presence and offer assistance to those who are adversely affected.

BIBLIOGRAPHY

Anthony, K. (2005). Counseling Problem Gamblers Online. *Counseling and Psychotherapy Journal* 16 (July), pp. 9-10.

Beucke, D. (2005). You Can Bet—But Don't Call It Gambling. *Business Week* 3851 (September 19), p. 14.

U.S. Shops Must Fold on Gaming. (2005). *Advertising Age* 76 (July 11), p. 8.

Online Protests

The Internet changed the way people communicate with the advent of e-mail, discussion boards, and Usenet groups. By the same token it changed the way organizations stay in touch with members. The so-called "Battle in Seattle" showcased the success of protesters and the failure of the World Trade Organization as far as new communication is concerned. While the WTO and the city of Seattle both employed poor planning and organization leading up to and during the 1999 conference, protesters demonstrated not only their ire, but also the power of mass communication centered on a cause. Indeed the protestors joined together to disrupt the WTO conference for a variety of causes, ranging from the protection of sea turtles to the labor rights of workers in underdeveloped countries. What the protesting groups had in common was a fear and dislike of globalization. Ironically, the dissidents bonded by means of global communication. According to Briggs (2002), each of the disparate groups wanting to make itself heard regarding issues addressed at the WTO had its own Web site. E-mail and message boards were used to bring protesters together for a mass demonstration. The exchange of plans and information allowed activists to coordinate the mass protests that paralyzed both the World Trade Organization and the city of Seattle, and focused the world's attention on the events.

The online activity led to street demonstrations that were extremely disruptive and in some cases violent. In addition to mass gatherings in the street, activists used the Internet for disruption of targeted sites and services. They posted fake Web sites that closely resembled the WTO site and announced that the conference had been cancelled. They staged mass dial-ins to bring down the official Web site. Most dramatic, though, was the action in the streets. The effect was that the conference ended in an impasse.

Because of the "Battle of Seattle," other protests have followed the same *modus operandi*. Indeed, using a search engine such as Google, one can type in the word "protests" and get any number of links to protests around the world, with schedules and descriptions. Protest.net (http://www.protest.net) serves as a clearing house for upcoming events. This Web site also offers an Activists Handbook, a listing of issues one might want to protest. Indians protesting dams in the Narmada River Valley have gained support from human rights and environmentalists worldwide through their Internet activism. An organization called IRN, the International Rivers Network (www.irn .org), seeks to protect rivers worldwide, from the Narmada to the Amazon to the Zambezi. Greenpeace, well known for zealous environmental activism, includes Internet communication in its ongoing crusades. Other groups have studied the success of those presently using global communication and are following suit.

At the same time, established institutions and organizations are working to prevent debacles such as the Seattle protests. They are more cognizant of the need for increased transparency and communication with activist groups. Because such groups often thrive on college campuses, university officials are increasingly sensitive to the possibility of protests from groups objecting to such things as investments in stocks in companies with poor human rights records. They are also moving away from purchasing goods with school logos from companies known for "sweatshop" production.

In today's increasingly complex and global society, both establishments and protest groups have learned the power of online communication. The ways in which they interact in the future will continue to evolve.

BIBLIOGRAPHY

Briggs, W. (2002). Sea Turtles, Cell Phones, and the WTO. *Communication World* 17 (February/March), pp. 13-14.

Baldi, S. (2000). The Internet for International and Social Protest: the Case of Seattle. *Research Paper No. 3, Policy planning Unit of the Ministry of Foreign Affairs of Italy, Roma.* Available at http://hostings.diplomacy.edu/baldi/italy.

McPherson, M. and Schapiro, M. (2001). When Protests Proceed at Internet Speed. *Chronicle of Higher Education,* 47 (March 23), p. B24.

Online Pyramid Schemes

Pyramid schemes involve the solicitation of a new member to an organization with the assurance that a significant amount of money can be made for a minimal amount of investment. Once a person has paid the initial fee, he or she must recruit others to join and pay similar admission fees. In truth the organizers of the scheme often have no product and, in order for the scheme to remain in place, new recruits must constantly be added. Pyramids are illegal.

Pyramids exist in many forms and some of these involve schemes that have been made possible using Internet resources. Fraudulent users may send potential victims e-mail messages that offer an array of options for making easy money. Common online schemes offer such options as the possibility to work at home performing such chores as home assembly, envelope stuffing, or data entry. People who respond to the e-mail and participate often don't get their money once the work is done or, more commonly, are required to recruit others before money can be received.

One simple online scheme requests that an e-mail recipient send a specified amount of money to the first person on a list and to add his or her own name at the bottom. Such schemes offer the assurance that when the user's name moves to the top of the list, that the recipient will receive large sums of money. In practice, this could only happen if new participants solicit additional members.

BIBLIOGRAPHY

Coward, C. (1998). How to Spot a Pyramid Scheme: Beware of Friends Who Hook You into Selling Get-Rich-Quick Products. *Black Enterprise* 28(7), p. 200.

Loza, E. (2001). Internet Fraud: Federal Trade Commission Prosecutions of Online Conduct. *Communications and the Law* 23(2), p. 55.

Rohan, R. F. (1998). How to Spot an Internet Hoax. *Black Enterprise* 28(11), p. 64.

Wells, J. T. (2000). So That's Why It's Called a Pyramid Scheme. *Journal of Accountancy* 190(4), p. 91.

Patriot Act

The Patriot Act (formally the USA PATRIOT Act), a bill signed by President George W. Bush on October 26, 2001, as a reaction to the September 11, 2001, attacks on the World Trade Center buildings in New York City and the Pentagon in Washington, DC, gave the United States Justice Department far-reaching powers in obtaining information and in detaining those suspected of certain types of crimes. The act allows government agencies to intercept and record phone calls and e-mail exchanges of suspected terrorists and foreign agents with greater ease. Using the power created by the Patriot Act, those enforcing the act may put non-U.S. citizens suspected of terrorist acts into prison indefinitely and may do so without trial and without providing counsel.

At the time of its passage, the act received tremendous support in both federal legislative branches with 357 members of the House voting for its passage and sixty-six voting against. In the Senate, ninety-eight senators voted for the Patriot Act and only one voted against.

Since its passage, a growing number of municipal governing bodies and state legislatures have raised concerns about the Patriot Act. Critics express concerns about the far-reaching power exercised by the federal government in gathering information and detaining suspected terrorists. Four states, Hawaii, Alaska, Maine, and Vermont, have passed resolutions condemning the act as have the cities of New York, Los Angeles, Dallas, Philadelphia, and Chicago. Criticism of the Patriot Act has come from both liberal and conservative sides of the political spectrum.

In addition to the authority to garner information from e-mail, the Patriot Act allows a government official from such agencies as the Federal Bureau of Investigation to approach a judge in the For-

Cybersins and Digital Good Deeds
© 2007 by The Haworth Press, Inc. All rights reserved.
doi:10.1300/5632_15

The Patriot Act allows a government official from such agencies as the Federal Bureau of Investigation to approach a judge in the Foreign Intelligence Surveillance Court and obtain a court order requiring librarians to produce a list of the books read by suspected individuals. (*Source:* © iStockphoto.com/Rusyanto, Paulus, "Woman Reading a Book." Available at http//:www.istockphoto.com.)

eign Intelligence Surveillance Court and obtain a court order requiring librarians to produce a list of the books read by suspected individuals. Once the list is obtained, a gag order prevents the librarian from telling anyone that the FBI has come to take the book list.

The original Patriot Act was scheduled to expire in December, 2005; however, a renewed version passed both legislative bodies and was signed by President Bush in March, 2006. The renewed version contained concessions made for critics concerned that the Patriot Act violated certain civil liberties.

BIBLIOGRAPHY

Abdolian, L. F. and Takooshian, H. (2003). The USA PATRIOT Act: Civil Liberties, the Media, and Public Opinion. *Fordham Urban Law Journal* 30(4), pp. 1429-1454.

Hentoff, N. (2002). The FBI Can Find Out What You Read. *Free Inquiry* 22(3), (Summer), pp. 13-14.

Phishing

Phishing, the practice of convincing Internet users to provide personal account information, social security numbers, credit card numbers, or personal identification numbers for fraudulent purposes, takes it name from the word *fishing,* the sport of providing bait that will be accepted by a number of receptive fish. Phishing begins with an e-mail being sent to a large group of people. The e-mail appears to come from a legitimate company and requests that recipients go to a Web site to update their account information. The e-mail is sent with the anticipation that at least a portion of those receiving the message will have a legitimate account with the identified company such as a bank or online payment service.

When the recipient of the e-mail goes to the phishing site, the Web site may look authentic and may bear the logo of the company. The text included on the hyperlinks on the Web site may too seem authentic; however, the links carry the user to a page with forms requesting information about the user's personal accounts. If the user completes the information, that information is sent, unbeknownst to the user, not to the legitimate company but to someone who will use the information to create new accounts or to access the victim's established ones.

Users should be cautious about providing updated electronic information prompted by an e-mail request. If the request seems to be bogus, a call to the company is worth the time.

BIBLIOGRAPHY

"FTC Finds Identity Theft Widespread." (2003). *The Washington Times* (September 4), p. A01.

"Internet Scammers Go 'Phishing'; Steal Personal Information by Imitating Legit Web Sites." (2003). *The Washington Times* (July 22), p. A01.

O'Sullivan, O. (2003). Gone 'Phishing': This Was the Summer When Consumers Were Lured to Fake Bank Websites with a View to Defrauding Them. *ABA Banking Journal* 95(11), pp. 7-8.

"Service Can Stop 'Phishing' for ID." (2003). *The Washington Times* (November 11), p. C08.

Phreaking

In the beginning the term *phreaking* was applied to the cracking of a telephone network to make free long-distance calls. Thanks to an article published in a Bell Systems technical manual in the mid-1960s, it was discovered that Bell Systems electronic switchers let calls go through when a 2600Hz tone (two octaves above the high E string on a guitar) was detected. Electronics engineers, students, and hobbyists, including Steve Jobs and Steve Wozniak (founders of Apple Computer), capitalized on such information by creating devices that produced a sound pitch at 2600Hz. It was soon also discovered that the toy whistles given away as prizes in Cap'n Crunch cereal boxes produced a 2600Hz tone (Wozniak). Using these whistles and boxes, phreakers, as they became known, could produce tones that would take hold of a telephone line and allow them to dial freely across the network.

Today the term is often applied to activities aimed at breaking the security of a network (Whatis?com, 2001). Modern phreaks have found interest in targeting and taking advantage of newer technologies and communications features, including Voice Over IP, and Caller ID. Despite constant system and security upgrades, phreaks continue to find new ways to exploit systems in the digital age.

BIOLOGRAPHY

Rosenblum, R. (1971). Secrets of the Blue Box. *Esquire Magazine* (October).

Whatis?com. Phreak. Available at http://searchsecurity.techtarget.com/sdefinition/0.290660.sid14_gci212783,00.html. Accessed June 27, 2006.

Wozniak, S. Letters—General Questions Answered. Available at http://www.woz.org/letters/general/03.html. Accessed September 19, 2005.

Plagiarism

Plagiarism involves using either the words or ideas of another person without giving credit to that person. Plagiarism violates the right of intellectual property, the notion that what one creates belongs to him or her and that the created property has value and should be protected by law.

As the notion of intellectual property became accepted, academia faced a daunting challenge to ascertain that the words and ideas used by students were not borrowed from others and, if they were, to formalize a citation standard for identifying the property owner. Near the turn of the twentieth century, the Modern Language Association (MLA) developed a set of citation formats requiring writers who used the text or ideas of others to identify the author and work of the original creation. The MLA citation standards are used today by authors writing in the liberal arts fields and in other disciplines. Other citation formats have evolved such as the American Psychological Association standards used today by many schools of education.

The issue of plagiarism has been complicated by the presence of the Internet. Schools have noted two particular problems. First, the ease of copying information directly from the Internet allows students to copy and paste text verbatim into their homework assignments, and students often do so without providing proper citations. In addition, students also may purchase papers from online paper mills and submit those papers to teachers as their own.

Teachers have developed resources to thwart the efforts of students who copy from the Internet. These resources include Web sites that allow teachers to compare a student's work with Internet resources. (See Turnitin.com)

Because students may easily plagiarize text from the Internet, teachers should be alerted to the need to teach respect for intellectual property, to make clear to the students the penalties for violating intellectual rights, and to teach both electronic and nonelectronic citation formats. In a larger sense every teacher should teach students to respect the sanctity of ideas and to cherish a regard for how important it is that those who create ideas are acknowledged for their creation.

BIBLIOGRAPHY

Dempsey, J. et al. (2004). WEB WATCH: Copyright and Plagiarism. *Phi Delta Kappan* 85(8), p. 630.

Dyrli, O. E. (2000). Confronting Online Plagiarism. *Matrix: The Magazine for Leaders in Higher Education* (October), p. 19.

Freedman, M. P. (2004). A Tale of Plagiarism and a New Paradigm. *Phi Delta Kappan* 85(7), p. 545.

Gibelman, M., Gelman, S. R., and Fast, J. (1999). The Downside of Cyberspace: Cheating Made Easy. *Journal of Social Work Education* 35(3), p. 367.

Rajala, J. (2002). Citation & Plagiarism. *T H E Journal* 30(4), p. 32.

Vernon, R. F., Bigna, S., and Smith, M. L. (2001). Plagiarism and the Web. *Journal of Social Work Education* 37(1), p. 193.

Wilhoit, S. (1994). Helping Students Avoid Plagiarism. *College Teaching* 42(4), pp. 161-164.

Podcasting

Podcasting refers to the process of creating a multimedia presentation and posting the presentation to a Web site where it may be downloaded or streamed to a user. The term was reportedly first used in September 2004 as a combination of the words *iPod* and *broadcasting*; however, neither an iPod nor any other digital player is required for receiving the files available from a podcast (Wikipedia .org). The file may be played directly on a computer using such resources as Windows Media Player.

Podcasting works like this. First, an audio or video recording is created and uploaded to a webserver. The completed product is then posted to a Web site, typically through a feed or list of available programs. The potential user then subscribes to the feed and receives the presentation. The entire file may be sent to the user or it may be streamed to the user in buffered segments. Because of its flexibility, there is speculation that podcasting may become popular for delivering current radio and video programs so that listeners may listen to a program at any time they choose.

Podcasters, as the users are sometimes called, use *podcasting* to share such audio presentations as original music, radio dramas, news reports, or issues-focused conversations. Educators are also looking at the capability of podcasting as another way to deliver instruction on the Internet.

BIBLIOGRAPHY

IPodder.org: The resource for the IPod Platform. Available at http://www.ipodder .org. Accessed July 31, 2006.

Wikipedia.org. Podcasting. Available at http://en.wikipedia.org/wiki/Podcasting. Accessed July 31, 2006.

Privacy and the Internet

You are in your home office or living room surfing the Web with your wireless laptop while watching television. Surely you are safe in the privacy of your own home. Surfing the net is like walking down a public street. Most Web sites use small programs called "cookies" that are downloaded onto a computer hard drive and then track the sites that the user visits, sending this information to Web site administrators. This is usually done for marketing, but it would not take much to make this a malicious activity. In June 2001, a report by the Department of Defense (DOD) revealed that more than 25 percent of the DOD Web sites sampled have no posted privacy statements and may still gather data on visitors, despite three previous directives to remove intrusive cookies and Web bugs from federal government sites. These sites may have also inadvertently let civilian companies obtain and later sell usage information the sites had collected.

Most Internet browsers now allow users to turn cookies off. That is, denying a cookie download when a user visits a site. This may cause the site to not be displayed, so browsers have incorporated an "ask me first" function. This functionality, which will also be used in other privacy areas, asks the user if it is okay to download a cookie from a visited site. This is worthwhile if the site is trusted.

Sending an e-mail is like sending a postcard. Anyone that comes into contact with that postcard can read it without your knowledge or permission. Pretty Good Privacy (PGP) is one of the oldest methods of protecting e-mail. PGP encrypts e-mail at the user's computer using the recipient's public key (see Encryption). When the recipient receives the e-mail, the software decrypts the message using a secret private key. This does require that both parties install and use PGP.

Junk e-mail, or spam, is the most common tool in the loss of online privacy. Experts say that consumers should not respond to spam e-mail in any way, and especially not by clicking on the "to remove from list" links. More often than not, these links merely help the spammer confirm that your address is active.

Shopping online allows for the greatest risk. Web sites take personal information such as names, addresses, telephone numbers, and credit card numbers to use themselves, sell to other operations, or sometimes have it stolen from them. Although credit card companies will usually cover unauthorized charges, users should be careful of where they shop. As in the real world, we have to trust someone. We just need to make sure that we trust the sites we are giving our information to.

BIBLIOGRAPHY

Arrison, S. (2002). How You Can Protect Your Privacy. *Consumers' Research Magazine* 85(2) (February), pp. 10-13, 24.

Bell, M. A. et al. (2004). Privacy. *Internet and Personal Computing Fads.* Binghamton, NY: Haworth Press, pp. 157-158.

Brandt, A. (2001) Who's Snooping on You? *PC World* 19(9) (September), p. 49.

Department of Defense (DOD) Office of the Inspector General (2001). Audit Report DOD Internet Practices and Policies (D-2001-130), p. 9.

Protecting Your Privacy. (2001) *Fortune* 142(12) (Winter), pp. 27-28.

Project Gutenberg

Project Gutenberg began in 1971 when an operator's account with 100 million dollars worth of computer time was given by the operators of the Xerox Sigma V mainframe at the Materials Research Lab at the University of Illinois to Michael Hart. The idea behind this was to give global access to books in electronic form. This holds true even today with over 17,000 electronic texts available free online (Project Gutenberg, 2006). These documents are formatted in ASCII code, which can be read by almost any computer and electronic book device. The advantage to the ASCII format is the absence of complicated formatting, which takes up much less space on a disk or in memory. This is important in archiving documents with limited space as well as allowing a user to take more information away from the library, be it on a floppy disk, CD, USB flash drive, or electronic book device. In fact, *Moby Dick,* a 600-page text, is stored at 65 kilobytes on the project Gutenberg Website. With documents of this size, an electronic book could contain a small, portable library as compared to about ten of the proprietary format of commercial electronic books (VanRoekel, 2000).

BIBLIOGRAPHY

Project Gutenberg. Available at http://www.gutenberg.org. Accessed July 17, 2006.

Van Roekel, J. L. (2000). Electronic Books: Portable Access to Digital Information. In Achleitner, H and Dimchev, A. (Eds.), *Libraries in the Age of the Internet.* Sofia, Bulgaria: ULISO.

RFID

Radio Frequency Identification is a technology built into computer chips that broadcasts a signal, much like an airplane transponder, that allows tracking. RFID is typically used in transportation and shipping tracking. For example, Wal-Mart utilizes RFID to track shipments from their distribution centers to individual stores; even so far as to individual packages. RFID chips are also widely used in automatic toll systems.

United Airline pilots and crews have been flying with passports equipped with RFID. The chips store personal information such as name, date of birth, and a digitized photo of the holder. To prevent counterfeiting or alterations to the passport, these chips can only be written to once (Single, 2005a).

Likewise Visa is proposing a new "contactless" system—consumers need only wave credit and debit cards within a few inches of a reader to complete a purchase. The technology is to be more convenient for merchants and consumers in reducing checkout times and lines by not requiring signatures of debit codes. Although this technology allows for ease and convenience of tracking and identification, there has been some controversy as well.

Digital Angel has been developing chips that are implanted under the skin of animals; whether pets or livestock: "pet identification using its patented FDA-approved implantable microchips; livestock identification and tracking using visual and RFID ear tags" (Digital Angel). The controversy lies in the use of the implants with humans. VeriChip, a subsidiary of Applied Digital (Digital Angel), has developed the first FDA-cleared, human-implantable RFID microchip to the only patented active RFID tag with skin-sensing capabilities. They market the chip in infant and patient protection, wander prevention, and access control.

Privacy activists are concerned that the unchecked use of RFID could negatively affect consumer privacy by allowing retailers to

Cybersins and Digital Good Deeds
© 2007 by The Haworth Press, Inc. All rights reserved.
doi:10.1300/5632_16

gather unprecedented amounts of information about consumer activity in their stores and link this information to customer information databases. These groups are also concerned with the possibility that companies, governments, and potential thieves may be able to monitor an individual's personal belongings, embedded with tiny RFID microchips, after they are purchased.

BIBLIOGRAPHY

Digital Angel. About Us. Available at http://www.digitalangelcorp.com/about.asp. Accessed July 21, 2006.

Gilbert, A. Privacy Advocates Call for RFID Regulation. *CNet News*. Available at http://news.com.com/2100-1029_3-5065388.html. Accessed July 21, 2006.

Gilbert, A. When Paying with Plastic, Why Swipe? Just Wave. *CNet News*. Available at http://news.zdnet.com/2100-9588_22-5589512.html. Accessed July 21, 2006.

Single, R. (2005a). Airline Tests RFID on the Fly. *Wired News* (August 9). Available at http://www.wired.com/privacy/0,1848,68451,00.html. Accessed July 21, 2006.

Single, R. (2005b). No Encryption for E-Passports. *Wired News* (February 24). Available at http://wired-vig.wired.com/news/privacy/0,1848,66686,00.html. Accessed July 21, 2006.

VeriChip Corporation. Available at http://www.verichipcorp.com. Accessed July 21, 2006.

Scare Chains

Spam and hoaxes are discussed elsewhere in this book, but the specific mention of a particularly irritating subset is hard to resist. Scare chains are those threatening e-mails that come with the instruction to "send on to X number of people or (fill in the blank with a horrible fate) will happen to you!" Letters that try to raise money through chain letters, or pyramid schemes, are illegal; scare chains are generally just annoying. They can range from sentimentality to gloom and doom. Some boast that they have been around the world any number of times, and indeed such claims may be true due to their longevity. It is not unusual to see the same chain recur year after year. A popular feature is the cute little picture made from keyboard characters. Examples include the Tweety Bird, in which a picture of Tweety is sent along with a promise that forwarding him will absolutely, positively bring immediate good luck.

Another type of scary spam is the letter issuing a frightening warning, often to women. Sometimes they can be racist in nature and, while they may be based on one time occurrences, the actual events likely happened years ago if at all. An example is a warning that went around after 9/11 cautioning people to avoid malls on Halloween that year because someone's friend from Afganistan warned that something terrible would happen on that date. This one caused so much publicity that some malls cancelled perfectly safe and innocent events because of the widespread panic.

Whether the message is a chirpy inspirational one asking you to send it on in order to receive a blessing or a scary one that threatens dire outcomes if you fail to forward, it can waste time and space and result in annoyance on the part of recipients. Good "netiquette," or

Cybersins and Digital Good Deeds
© 2007 by The Haworth Press, Inc. All rights reserved.
doi:10.1300/5632_17

computer etiquette, is to avoid posting scare chains or any other spam or chain e-mail, and to be the person to break the chain and not forward it if you do get one.

BIBLIOGRAPHY

Chain Letters. (2005). Available at http://hoaxbusters.ciac.org/HoaxBustersHome .html

Script Kiddies

Anyone who has logged on to a server at work or school and has been greeted with a silly or rude message has seen the work of a script kiddy. Often seen by themselves and others as rather harmless pranksters, script kiddies are hacker wannabes. They lack the expertise necessary to crack codes and break into networks themselves; instead they download programs from the Internet that enable them to gain access and scan files. Often the motivation is simple: just to see if they can succeed and then to see what they can see. In little Edcouch, Texas, deep in the Texas Rio Grande Valley, a sixth grader put into motion a script he obtained from a chat room and in minutes caused a brownout of all his school district's networks (Shields, 2003), thus illustrating the fact that such activities go beyond mere mischief. Scorned by real programmers, including hackers, script kiddies seek to make trouble by gaining easy access to unprotected sites.

Because they are looking for easy targets, script kiddies are very much a threat to the unwary home user. Often they use automated bot programs that ceaselessly work like perpetual motion machines, probing large blocks of IP addresses looking for entry points. Once a penetration is made, that computer can be taken over and used to attack others, unbeknownst to its owner. The spread of broadband connections has been a boon to those wanting to stage mass attacks because of increased access. While some script kiddies may just be playing games that they consider real-life alternatives to computer or video gaming, others may have more sinister goals such as gaining personal information, spreading computer viruses, or shutting down hard drives. Another reason script kiddies may be dangerous is that they get coerced into doing dirty work for criminals through challenges in chat rooms and online groups. Because they are less cautious or aware of the consequences of their actions, they may delve into networks and then share their findings with those who have more sinister motives. Clearly the actions of script kiddies, not to mention their more sophisticated hacker mentors, are not to be taken lightly.

What should one do to thwart intrusion by script kiddies, hackers, and all unwanted intruders? Just as homes need strong locks and commonsense security measures, computers should be secured by taking a few cautionary steps:

- Firewall software can be bought at minimal costs.
- If a user is curious about possible breaches in the past, he or she should visit a Web site called ShieldsUp (http://www.grc.com).
- Be aware of the blinking lights on your DSL or cable modem. If they constantly flicker even though you are not actively online, outside activity could be going on.
- Do not indiscriminately download files, including e-mail attachments.
- When you are not using your computer, turn it off. Leaving it on and idle all the time just increases vulnerability.

The old Scout motto, "Be Prepared," is still good advice, especially when it comes to computer security.

BIBLIOGRAPHY

Gibson, S. (2005) Shields Up! Available at http://www.grc.com. Accessed July 17, 2006.

Shields, C. (2003). Are Script Kiddies Hacking Into Your System? How to Fight the Onslaught of Cyber Attacks. *District Administration* 38 (November), pp. 54-56.

Tanaka, J. (2001). Don't Get Burned! *Newsweek* 138 (August 8), pp. 52-53.

Verton, D. (2001). Black Hat Highlights Real Danger of Script Kiddies. *Computerworld* 35 (August 23) pp. 7-8.

Slander, Libel, and Technology

Slander involves the use of the spoken word to defame the character of another person. Slander is in a sense the parallel of libel, the written defamation of another.

Slander or libel causes a loss of rights on the part of the victim by causing the victim to be perceived in some lesser way as a result of the statement made. If a person is accused of slander or libel and pursues the issue legally, a plaintiff must prove that as a result of being seen in a different or lesser way, there is some kind of economic or pecuniary loss resulting from the words spoken or written by the accused.

The issue of slander and libel has implications not only for individuals. Corporations involved in media such as a newspaper, publisher, or broadcaster may be sued for producing defaming information.

Recent technology advances have impacted the issues of slander and libel in several ways. First, technology creates a potentially far-reaching effect for slanderous or libelous statements as the Internet offers the ability to share those statements instantly to a worldwide audience.

In addition, the ability to alter graphics, sound, or text in a multimedia presentation adds another dimension to the study and understanding of slander and libel. (See Multimedia Manipulation.) If the alteration of original graphics, sound, or text is done in ways that prove injurious, then libel or slander may be involved.

BIBLIOGRAPHY

Barendt, E. (1997). *Libel and the Media: The Chilling Effect*. Oxford: Clarendon Press.

Barr, L. J. (2002). Use of False Light: A Barometer of News Media Performance? *Communications and the Law* 24(1), pp. 1-52.

Kim, G. H. and Paddon, A. R. (1999). Digital Manipulation as New Form of Evidence of Actual Malice in Libel and False Light Cases. *Communications and the Law* 21(3), p. 57.

Lidsky, L. B. (2000). Silencing John Doe: Defamation & Discourse in Cyberspace. *Duke Law Journal* 49(4), p. 855.

Mclean, D. (2002). Internet Defamation. *Communications and the Law* 24(4), pp. 21-42.

Social Engineering

All the firewalls and sophisticated security systems that an organization or company may employ will come to naught if the issue of human error and security is not addressed. In broad terms, social engineering means manipulating people to do your will. In reference to technology, the term describes deceiving users of targeted computer systems to divulge confidential information such as passwords, access codes, or account information. In some instances it is laughably easy to accomplish.

Probably the crudest example of finding information that is supposed to be private is through trash or dumpster diving. Simply using a shredder can protect against such items as memos, meeting notes, partial documents resulting from printer jams, account and credit card numbers, travel plans, employee names, etc. Other dangerous discards include old hard drives and lost or discarded disks, CDs, and flash drives. Educating employees about such dangers and instituting procedures for disposal of waste are important measures.

Slightly more sophisticated invasions involve attacking "wetware," a hacker term for human beings as opposed to hardware or software. Often it is as easy as making a few phone calls to access confidential information as opposed to hacking into a system. In fact, some individuals make their livings demonstrating this fact to managers. One scenario involved a man who did a little checking into a company directory for employee names. He then called people, addressed them personally, posed as a new-hire who had lost passwords and codes, and charmingly pled for assistance as he started out his new career. People obligingly shared, wanting to help the nice young man get off to a smooth start without getting into trouble with his superiors. In a matter of minutes the imposter had vital, supposedly confidential data. Help desks and receptionists are especially vulnerable, since they are trained to be accommodating and helpful.

Passwords are especially susceptible to threats by social engineers as well as hackers. Many people use the same password for multiple purposes, thus endangering numerous accounts through mishandling of that one simple word. Even though they have been warned for years about the danger of doing so, many people still keep passwords

All the firewalls and sophisticated security systems that an organization or company may employ will come to naught if the issues of human error and security are not addressed. (*Source:* © iStockphoto.com/Travis, Jaimie. "Business Meeting." Available at http//:www.istockphoto.com.)

close at hand, even posting them on computer monitors with sticky notes.

Use of obvious choices such as birthdates is another mistake that can backfire since such information can be obtained with relative ease.

Impersonation and persuasion are two of the most popular tools in social engineering. In the former, someone may pose as a repairperson, IT support person, or other individual with the right to know confidential information. With the latter, a con artist may come up with an engaging story, replete with flattery, that appeals to an employee's desire to be helpful.

The answer to social engineering is awareness. Home users need to be protective of passwords and discarded documents. Companies and organizations must invest in training, possibly using experts that specialize in computer security. Many times such individuals will evaluate a client by mock infiltration, then use the weaknesses revealed as valuable lessons. Regardless of the means, individuals, organizations and companies must be aware and vigilant regarding social engineering.

BIBLIOGRAPHY

Davis, R. (2004). Social Engineering. Texas Association for Educational Technology Conference, Ft. Worth, TX, November 5.

Seltzer, L. (2005) Tales of Professional Social Engineer. *PC Magazine* 24 (June 7), p. 102

Spam

Spam is unsolicited and often unwanted e-mail. Such e-mail is received in some form by most people who have e-mail accounts. The information received is generally of a commercial nature and offers some product or service. Spam may be equated with electronic junk mail.

The spam sender may obtain the e-mail address in a number of ways. The e-mail address of the spam recipient may be included in a group mailing and acquired either from other businesses or from a number of Internet ploys.

The volume of spam has increased dramatically the last few years and, because spam takes up substantial bandwidth, has negatively impacted more legitimate digital exchanges. In addition to its impact upon individuals and upon the business community, the effect of spam has also impacted schools by hindering more legitimate instructional uses.

President George W. Bush signed a federal anti-spam law, referred to as CAN-SPAM, in December 2003. The law became effective January 1, 2004. The law prevents sending e-mail with false information in subject lines and routing data and requires that the recipients have the capability of choosing not to receive subsequent e-mails from a particular e-mail address. Monetary fines and prison terms were defined for offenders, and provisions were outlined for more substantial penalties for repeat offenders.

Critics of the law point to the fact that the law doesn't prohibit sending spam, but rather makes its transmissions pass certain truth tests ("Spam Threat Called Manageable," 2003). Some states have attempted to pass more strenuous legislation limiting the creation and transmission of spam.

BIBLIOGRAPHY

"Bush Signs 1st Antispam Effort into Law; Outlaws Fake E-Mail, OKs 'Do-Not-E-Mail' List." (2003). *The Washington Times* (December 17), p. C09.

"Consider Revenge in the War on Spam." (2003). *The Washington Times* (January 21), p. C09.

de Jager, P. (2003). No Interest in Spam. *ABA Banking Journal* 95(6), p. 10.

Harris, K. (2004). Taking the Lid off the New CAN-SPAM Law. *ABA Banking Journal* 96(3), pp. 10,12.

Jennings, J. (2003). IT in a Time of Budget Cuts: How School Funding Will Affect the Quality of Education. *T H E Journal* 30(6), pp. 14-18.

"Spam Threat Called Manageable; Study Says Benefits Will Keep E-Mail a Force at Work." (2003). *The Washington Times* (October 6), p. A01.

Wren, C. (2003). Spam Wars: Battling the Relentless Web Tide. *Commonweal* (February), p. 16.

Splogs

First there was spam, then blogs, and now there is a new term for the evil child of these two Internet entities, splogs! Splogs are weblogs that are spammed, or sent out en masse, with the purpose of (what else?) advertising. A splog mimics a legitimate weblog in appearance and presence, but is actually fake and infested with ads. Because it is simple, cheap, and inviting to use Yahoo or Google and set up a personal weblog or blog, spammers and marketers can with equal ease as legitimate bloggers use the services to sell products. Therefore people may block spam in e-mail to get away from never-ending and annoying ads, only to have them pop up when they search for interesting and relevant blogs. According to Mills (2005), October 2005 saw what was termed a "splogsplosion," with thousands of fake sites appearing in just one weekend. Sploggers stuff their creations with fake keywords, using names of popular bloggers and topics that generate a lot of interest, and as a result bog down the search engines designed to look for blogs by subject. By fall 2005, close to 10 percent of all blogs created daily, or about 7,000, were in actuality splogs (Swartz, 2005). Google and Microsoft have both vowed to crack down on this fledgling technique of once again inundating people with unwanted commercial messages.

BIBLIOGRAPHY

Mills, E. (2005). Tempted by Blogs, Spam Becomes 'Splog.' *CNET News.com.* (October 20). Available at http://www.news.com. Accessed July 17, 2006.

Swartz, J. (2005). "November Spamalanche Bears Down on PC Users." *USA Today* (October 26).

Spoofing

There are different forms of spoofing. The first is IP spoofing in which unauthorized computer access is gained when an intruder sends messages including an IP address that indicates, by modifying packet headers, that the message is from a trusted host. Web spoofing creates a "shadow copy" of the entire Web. This copy is sent through the victim's computer while tracking all of the users activities on "the Web" including passwords, account numbers, or any other information that the victim may enter. A third example of spoofing is e-mail spoofing, which has actually happened to me (Van Roekel). E-mail spoofing occurs when a user receives an e-mail that appears to have originated from a source different from the source that it was actually from. In my instance, folks were getting spam e-mail from another source, but with my email address attached. This use of technology is very easy to implement. Several Web sites have scripted programs to allow for this (I won't list them here). Consequently, it is very difficult to track the true sender.

Because there is no way to prevent these types of attacks, the best protection is understanding these hacks and using cryptographic signatures to exchange authenticated e-mail messages. Also, check with your Internet service provider to see their policies and procedures for dealing with spoofing. At Sam Houston State University if the e-mail originates from campus the accounts and computers are shut down and disciplinary action is taken; if the e-mail originates from off campus, an e-mail is sent to abuse@domain.com and the offending address is blocked at the campus firewall.

BIBLIOGRAPHY

Felton, E.W., Balfanz, D., Dean, D., and Wallach, D.S. (1997). Secure Internet Programming: Web Spoofing: An Internet Con Game. Paper presented at the 20th National Information Systems Security Conference, Baltimore, Maryland. Available at http://www.cs.princeton.edu/sip/pub/spoofing.html. Accessed August 2, 2005.

Spoofed/Forged Email. CERT Coordination Center. Available at http://www.cert
  .org/tech_tips/ email_spoofing.html. Accessed August 2, 2005.
What is IP Spoofing? Webopedia Computer Dictionary. Available at http://www
  .webopedia.com/TERM/I/IP_spoofing.html. Accessed August 2, 2005.

Spyware or Adware

Information may be gathered from the computer of an Internet user without his or her consent. The information is gathered when a small software program that collectively goes by the term *spyware* or *adware* is placed, often without the user's consent, onto his or her workstation. The program is frequently delivered to the computer through the installation of freeware, shareware, or program updates, but the program may be added to a workstation by simply going to a certain Web site.

The purpose of the spyware is to track either Internet usage or workstation activity and to relay that information to others. Some spyware can capture the workstation user's keystrokes and record such information as social security numbers or charge account numbers. Other types gather information about e-mail accounts and passwords while less malicious applications use the gathered information to determine which pop-up ads or personal information the user will see when he or she accesses a certain Web site.

Excessive spyware on a computer can slow its processing speed. To counter the presence of excessive spyware, programs have been developed that allow it to be removed or monitored.

The information collected by spyware may be used for a malicious intent; however, some spyware called *cookies* determine which information to display when the user accesses a particular site. Some cookies store preferences making the return to the site easier to navigate. Other type of cookies store information about the sites visited so that the user will see specific types of advertising.

Cookies may be controlled within an Internet browser such as Netscape or Explorer by turning off the capability for a user to place a cookie onto a user's computer. Some Web sites, however, want cookies turned on so that information may be collected and will instruct the user to do so in order to use a Web site most productively.

BIBLIOGRAPHY

"How Spammers Exploit the News; Current Events Trigger Onslaught of E-Mail Ads." (2003). *The Washington Times* (October 14), p. A01.

Rajala, J. (2002). Web Site Filtering. *T H E Journal* 30(5), p. 30.

Rohan, R. (2003). Stop Pop-Up Pests and Spyware. *Black Enterprise* (July), p. 44.

Steganography

Steganography is the concealment of information within seemingly innocuous carriers. The term, derived from Greek, literally means covered writing. Think of it in these terms: in cryptography we try to protect our message content; in steganography we do not want anyone to know that the message is there.

The simplest technique of hiding information digitally is to replace the noise in an image or sound file with the message. A digital file consists of numbers that represent the intensity of light or sound at a particular point in time or space. Usually these numbers are computed in a way that can't be detected easily by humans. One spot in an image might have 220 units of blue on a scale that runs between 0 and 255 total units. An average eye would not notice if that one spot was converted to having 219 units of blue. If this process is done systematically, it is possible to hide large volumes of information just below the threshold of perception. A typical high-quality digital image has 2048 by 3072 pixels that each contain 24 bits of information about the colors of the image, which means that as much as 756K of data can be hidden. Peter Wayner (2002) asserts in this example that more information could be hidden than the text of his book. Terrorist watchers suspect Al Qaeda uses Internet steganography to deliver messages (Cohen, 2001).

An opposite example is watermarks. Often watermarks are meant to be seen (albeit barely). Authors of digital media often add hidden information to describe the restrictions on the file; i.e., expiration dates, copyright information, and the like. Watermarking, as opposed to steganography, has the additional condition of strength against possible attacks.

BIBLIOGRAPHY

Cohen, A. (2001). When terror hides online. *Time* 158(21) (November 12), p. 65.

Johnson, N. Steganography. Available at http://www.jjtc.com/stegdoc/steg1995.html. Accessed September 15, 2005.

Katzenbeisser, S. and Petitcolas, F. A. P. (Eds.) (2000). *Information hiding techniques for steganography and digital watermarking.* Boston: Artech House.

Wayner, P. (2002). *Disappearing Cryptography: Information Hiding: Steganography & Watermarking.* Boston: MK/Morgan Kaufmann Publishers.

Surfer's Voice

One person is talking on the phone to another, discussing a matter of great interest or concern. The other person responds in a flat, non-committal voice with vague responses such as "Right . . . Okay . . . uh huh. . . ." Then comes a tell-tale clue such as the sound of keyboard clicking or the happy little noise made when a solitaire game is concluded. It becomes clear that one party was only half listening while surfing the Internet, playing a game, or otherwise occupying himself or herself at the computer. This phenomenon has been given the name "surfer's voice."

Being on the receiving end of this sort of flawed communication is frustrating, if not insulting. Surfing or computing while talking is just another type of multitasking that is increasingly prevalent today. A related term, also discussed in this book, is *absent presence,* in which the individual with whom someone wants to communicate is showing only partial interest while also doing something else, particularly with a computer. While these lapses in courtesy are annoying, they are also tempting.

This is the age of multitasking, and many people think nothing of talking on the phone, instant messaging, and reading e-mail simultaneously. Of course there is the reality that doing several things at once often means nothing is done well. In this day of communication as well as information overload, it is important to maintain perspective and learn to prioritize our activities, including the ways we direct our attention.

BIBLIOGRAPHY

Berman, D. (2003). Technology Hodgepodge Adds to Life's Distractions. *The Wall Street Journal* (November 16), p. A7.

Gilster, P. (2004). "Time to Think is Lacking." *Raleigh NC News and Observer* (May 6), p. F1.

Sympathy Hoaxes

Most people are good-hearted and rise to situations of need publicized in the news and elsewhere. Alas, many people are also gullible. This combination of characteristics provides fertile ground for Internet hoaxers. Sometimes bogus sob stories get circulated widely via the Internet and eventually take on lives of their own as recipients send them on and bring them back to life time and time again.

The most famous example of an Internet sympathy plea, as described by Internet trainer Walt Howe, involved a young boy in the late 1980s who was suffering from a brain tumor and wanted to garner a Guinness World Record for receiving the most get-well cards. His plea went out over all types of media, and cards flooded in. He got so many, in fact, that it swamped mail services in his small town. As a result of the publicity, a philanthropist donated money and he underwent successful surgery. He is now a perfectly healthy young man in his twenties. But the cards keep pouring in, addressed to Craig Shergold, Sherwood, Sherwold and many other name variants. Craig and his family have issued numerous requests for the cards to stop. There is even a disclaimer at the Make-a-Wish Web site (www.wish.org). It appears that the story and its appeal has become too big and enduring to stop. Another story, also denied by the American Cancer Society, says that ACS will donate three cents to cancer research to everyone who sends the message on to new recipients. First, there would be no way for anyone to gather such data, and second, ACS repeatedly decries the use of its name in chain letters.

Regrettably, another story has attracted hoaxers, that of missing children. The Internet is an excellent way to get the word out about missing and abducted persons, but not all such alerts are valid. A wise course of action is to check the National Center for Missing & Exploited Children before passing on such a plea for assistance.

Another variation on this theme is described by Howe as "warm fuzzy stories for good luck." These involve chain e-mail messages again, this time telling a heartwarming or inspirational story with the instructions to send it on to a stated number of people for good luck. Sometimes the admonition is included that failure to send will bring bad fortune. Chain letters waste time and bandwidth and wear on the nerves of recipients. Good luck and best wishes to all who break the chains!

BIBLIOGRAPHY

Hayden, T. (2002). Gotcha! *Time* 133 (September 2), p. 30.
Howe, W. Sympathy Hoaxes and Warm Fuzzy Stories. Walt's Navigating the Net Forum. Available at http://www.walthowe.com. Accessed July 17, 2006.

Technology and Knowledge Management

As an institution attempts to transform itself into a technology-based institution, and as knowledge management becomes more vital to that institution, information technology and its infrastructure can provide relevant, timely, and accurate information, from a centralized place, to anyone who needs it. Although the definitions are legion, knowledge management may be defined as a systematic and integrative process of coordinating institution-wide activities of acquiring, creating, storing, sharing, diffusing, developing, and deploying information by individuals and groups toward institutional goals and the ability to utilize data within the constructs of a situation within these goals. In thinking about the development of a knowledge management infrastructure, the greatest component in assessment, planning and purchasing, instruction, and implementation of information technology, is education. Using technology tools, with these objectives, assists in getting to the heart of how the institution sees itself handling knowledge management now and in the future. This process will answer the questions of how the institution plans on utilizing the technology before it is purchased, and whether the technology is upgradeable and expandable. As with any project, using the right tool for the right job is key. It will also answer questions of utilizing the technology for future plans. Collecting authoritative information not only on the technology, but on how the technology is to be used, greatly enhances the user's skills in thinking about the project. Those involved begin thinking of the technology and its utilization in context-free situations, while recognizing meaningful elements of application toward a greater competence. Once the assessment has gotten underway, it is vital to the project to find those who want to utilize the technology and are sold on the idea. This is an imperative step as selling the idea of use to others will depend on members of the institution

doi:10.1300/5632_18

who are not directly involved with the planning stages. In preparing an institution for the utilization of an information-technology-based knowledge management system, education is the key component in each step of the process. Getting users to think about the process, the system, and the way the system will be used well before and during the planning stages will assure greater and better utilization after the system is in place.

BIBLIOGRAPHY

Rastogi, P. N. (2000). Knowledge Management and Intellectual Capital—The New Virtuous Reality of Competitiveness. *Human Systems Management* 19, pp. 39-49.

Van Roekel, J. L. (2002). Knowledge Management and Information Technology: Educating Users from Assessment to Implementation. *Perspectives in Higher Education* 11, pp. 228-231.

Technolust

Technolust is a coined word that describes the ever-increasing desire to possess the latest in electronic gadgetry—the more the better. A little lust of this type is not necessarily bad, providing the consumer can afford the purchases and disposes of rejected devices responsibly. For many people, being early adopters who like to try new gizmos and applications is a rewarding pastime. It can become problematical, though, if the drive for the newest and latest causes people, companies, and institutions to neglect other priorities.

In his books *Silicon Snake Oil* (1995) and *High Tech Heretic* (1999), Clifford Stoll decries the tendency of individuals, businesses, and schools to go after all things electronic, wasting limited time and money on technologies that are not user friendly and may be less efficient than the low-tech processes and practices they seek to replace. He also questions the belief that technology aids communication and contends that, to the contrary, it can isolate people. Face-to-face contact in business, he says, is irreplaceable. Many people will agree that their clogged computer mail boxes and the time spent dealing with e-mail are barriers to productivity. As in most things, a balance between excess and outright rejection of technology is necessary.

Nowhere is such a balance more needed than in the field of education. School administrators love to talk about the computer/student ratio and show off the latest in educational hardware and software. Interactive whiteboards are fun and attractive, but they are no replacement for dynamic teachers. Parents often seem more concerned about the number of computers than the number and quality of library books or other valuable resources. E-books and online resources are great for providing information, but are useless without assignments that promote critical thinking. Computer-aided instruction often adds up to little more than electronic flash cards. Far too often, computers and other gadgets are purchased and thrust into classrooms and labs, with little or no training provided to educators. Teachers, who are already laden with other responsibilities, find little time or incentive to learn basic operation, must less effective and challenging practices for using the technologies with their students.

BIBLIOGRAPHY

Stephens, M. (2004). Technoplans vs. Technolust. *Library Journal* 129 (November 1), pp. 36-37.

Stoll, C. (1995). *Silicon Snake Oil.* New York: Doubleday.

Stoll, C. (1999). *High Tech Heretic.* New York: Doubleday.

Stoll, C. (2005). Cliff Stoll's Home Page. Available at http://www.ocf.berkeley.edu/~stoll. Accessed July 17, 2006.

Trojan Horses

A Trojan horse is a small computer program that is embedded in another program. A Trojan horse often bears the name of legitimate software. When the program is installed on a workstation or server, the results can play havoc for users. Trojan horses are often contained in downloaded software updates and patches. Trojan horses do not automatically replicate like worms, but they can be just as destructive.

Because a Trojan horse bears a legitimate name, the user believes that its installation will offer some unique capability. In reality the Trojan horse can invade the workstation or server operating system and cause such behavior as allowing information to flood the system and slow down or incapacitate the network.

An understanding of the myth behind the term *Trojan horse* provides insight into the use of the term and into its application in modern technology. The Trojan horse software takes its name from the Greek myth surrounding the abduction of Helen, wife of King Menelaus of Sparta, by Paris of Troy. Helen is taken to Troy located on the western coast of present day Turkey and a war breaks out. The war was brought to an end when Greeks hiding inside a wooden horse were unknowingly brought inside the walls of Troy leading to the defeat of the Trojans. Thus, computer programs that are hidden inside of other programs, updates, or patches bear the name *Trojan horse* suggesting that something unknown and destructive to its user is included inside.

Several practices are important in avoiding Trojan horses including keeping frequent backups, being cautious about Internet downloads and e-mail attachments, and installing an effective software virus protection program.

BIBLIOGRAPHY

Bytes for Beginners. (2001). *NEA Today* (November), p. 35.

Gozzi, R., Jr. (2000). The Trojan Horse Metaphor. *ETC: A Review of General Semantics* 57(1), p. 80.

Jacobson, H. and Green, R. (2002). Computer Crimes. *American Criminal Law Review* 39(2), pp. 273-325.

Smith, L. M., and McDuffie, R. S. (1994). Defending against Computer Viruses. *The CPA Journal* 64(8), pp. 74-75.

Turnitin.com

The rationale for the creation of Turnitin.com, an Internet Web site, was developed in 1996 at the University of California at Berkeley in response to a need by professors to prevent plagiarism by students using Internet resources. From that beginning, the Turnitin.com Web site was created and has grown to provide a number of instructional services for teachers including plagiarism recognition, a site for student collaboration projects and the ability to mark student papers online and to store teacher grades. The heart of the Turnitin.com service, however, is the plagiarism recognition capability.

The plagiarism recognition resource works by allowing teachers to submit a student's paper and to use the software to compare the paper with a database containing millions of other student papers. In addition the paper is compared with a content database containing billions of pages of Internet data (Turnitin.com). The result of the comparison is returned to the teacher with any suspected plagiarism highlighted and linked to the source. The teacher then makes the final decision regarding whether plagiarism has occurred.

The use of Turnitin.com has expanded beyond the traditional classroom by interfacing its service with that of popular course management software programs used by colleges and universities to deliver courses online. Using Turnitin.com via the course management software allows online teachers to catch plagiarized papers as face-to-face teachers do.

BIBLIOGRAPHY

Freedman, M. P. (2004). A Tale of Plagiarism and a New Paradigm. *Phi Delta Kappan* 85(7), p. 545.

Green, M. (2000). 'TurnItIn' Snares Online Cheaters. *NEA Today* (April), p. 22.

Rittschof, K. A. and Griffin, B. W. (2003). Confronting Limitations of Cyberspace College Courses: Part 2—Developing Solutions. *International Journal of Instructional Media* 30(3), pp. 285-294.

Scanlon, P. M. (2003). Student Online Plagiarism: How Do We Respond? *College Teaching* 51(4), pp. 161-165.

Vernon, R. F., Bigna, S., and Smith, M. L. (2001). Plagiarism and the Web. *Journal of Social Work Education* 37(1), p. 193.

Typosquatting

One way to get to a desired Internet Web site is to key the URL into the browser's address line. This can be a quick one-step method, but only if the user does not miskey or misspell any component of the address. If a mistake is made, the user may find himself or herself at another site entirely, and often one that is quite an unpleasant surprise.

The likelihood of this happening has inspired webmasters who want to capitalize on such mistakes to put up sites, often pornographic, with addresses similar to well-known and popular locations. This practice has come to be known as typosquatting, or the use of misleading domain names. One tactic is to post a site with an address identical to another's except for the last letters, or domain name. Thus the infamous whitehouse.com, which was once a pornographic site, duped users who wanted to go to the United States White House site whitehouse.gov. A third "whitehouse" site, www.whitehouse.org, looks very much like the official location but is satirical in nature.

Another way to trick people into visiting a site is to register it with an address that contains a common misspelling of another popular site. At one time such misspellings as www.teltubbies.com and www.bobthebiulder.com would bring up porn sites. Both of these tactics were addressed by the PROTECT Act (Prosecutorial Remedies and Other Tools to end the Exploitation of Children Today), which was enacted April 30, 2003. This act made it illegal to deceive a minor into visiting a site by employing a URL that was purposely similar to another location. The infamous whitehouse.com site became a page advertising house paint, and other sites faded away. It is still a good idea to be vigilant about misleading domains and pornography though, because such sites appear and disappear very quickly.

One other, and legal, use of misleading domains is luring people to intended sites for reasons other than pornography, especially advertising. Thus the whitehouse site became a commercial for exterior paint. If you key in "bobbuilder" instead of "bobthebuilder" today, a site selling toys of another brand appears.

How can these misleading sites be avoided? Wise domain holders will often buy derivative spellings for their sites as well, but it may be hard to think of all of them. Careful users should bookmark, copy, and paste URLs, and use browsers to locate sites. Parents and educators should be extra careful to teach children to access sites by these means rather than keying in addresses.

BIBLIOGRAPHY

Sullivan, B. (2000). 'Typosquatting' Turns Flubs into Cash. ZDNet News (September 22). Available at http://news.zdnet.com. Accessed July 17, 2006.

Virtual Offices

Now that people are going wireless with computers, PDAs, cell phones, webcams, and other devices, it is increasingly possible to work from home. For at least a decade, the future of the cubicle as a workplace has been debated. The need to physically report to a given location in order to do one's job is less and less a necessity. It is not unusual to see people working on airplanes, in coffee shops, in parks, and in other public places, especially locations where wireless service is available.

Working at home or in other environments rather than the traditional office is enticing to lots of employees and employers alike. Employees can save on the considerable fuel costs resulting from commuting and possibly be at home for children or other loved ones needing care. Employers can save on facility and utility costs, and likely hope for increased productivity as people reclaim time lost to commuting as well as flexibility of choice in work time. Anytime-anywhere computing is here to stay, and the workplace will never be the same.

Although some may view this trend toward being able to work from almost anywhere as a wonderful thing, others voice doubts. The same ubiquity that allows one to work anywhere at any time also means that it is nearly impossible to escape the demands and stresses of one's job. E-mail and cell phone calls can follow the hapless vacationer even if he or she vows not to be distracted by work. Measuring people's pay by the number of hours they accrue will become much harder when the lines between home and work become increasingly blurred. People who do work from home will attest that it is very difficult to separate one's home life from work. Workaholics will have even less chance of finding it possible to get away. When the workplace is just a few steps away from the kitchen or family room, it becomes challenging to keep a balance between personal and work life. This challenge is one that many will need to overcome in the near future, because the ubiquity of work is a trend which will not reverse but rather increase in the future.

BIBLIOGRAPHY

Edwards, C. (2005). Wherever You Go, You're On the Job. *Business Week* 3938 (June 20), pp. 87-90.

Viruses and Virus Protection

In the world of the Internet the term *virus* has come to refer to a small program that runs on a computer without the consent of the operator. The virus attacks the operation of the computer creating a number of possible harmful results. Viruses often affect the computer's operating system; however, viruses may also impact the operation of specific software. The effect of viruses can include simple things such as displaying a silly message on the screen to a more serious act such as reformatting the hard drive or preventing the opening of certain programs.

Viruses often come from CDs, floppy disks, e-mail attachments, and downloaded programs. Once a virus is in place on a computer, the virus may be transmitted throughout a network. The more sophisticated viruses can get through security efforts such as firewalls.

Some viruses operate separately of any file and duplicate themselves again and again, impacting the performance of the computer by taking up memory space. Some debate exists as to whether these viruses should instead be identified with the term *worm* (see Worm). Other virus software bears a legitimate name and is buried within the operation of a legitimate program (see Trojan Horse).

The monetary and productivity loss caused by viruses on the Internet has prompted legislation aimed at halting their spread. The Computer Fraud and Abuse Act of 1986 addressed viruses spread by individuals. Other acts, such as the National Information Infrastructure Protection Act of 1996 as amended by the Patriot Act, outline certain types of offenses and punishment for individuals who might tamper with or impact the integrity of government files.

Virus protection software aimed at protecting computer workstations and servers from attack is available for a modest price. Because those who create viruses are constantly creating new, evasive, and more powerful versions, virus software must constantly be updated. Network operators often choose to download virus protection updates automatically to the server and to load the updates onto all network workstations.

BIBLIOGRAPHY

Glanz, W. (2000). "Virus Infects E-Mail Networks." *The Washington Times* 5 (May 5), p. 1.

Graham, L. D. (1999). *Legal Battles That Shaped the Computer Industry.* Westport, CT: Quorum Books.

Hunton, J. E. (1998). Facts and Fables about Computer Viruses. *Journal of Accountancy* 185(5), p. 39.

Jacobson, H. and Green, R. (2002). Computer Crimes. *American Criminal Law Review* 39(2), p. 273.

Nicholson, L. J., Shebar, T. F, and Weinberg, M. R.. (2000). Computer Crimes. *American Criminal Law Review* 37(2), p. 207.

Warchalking

Popularized by Londoner Matt Jones on his now-defunct blog in 2002, warchalking is the marking of sidewalks and walls to identify open wireless network hotspots. Three symbols are used to indicate availability: a circle indicates a closed wireless network, two half-moons back to back denote a wireless network that has been generously or inadvertently left open, and a circle with a "W" in the middle indicates a Wired Equivalent Privacy (WEP) encrypted node.

It is still debated whether this is an illegal activity. While it is understood that stealing documents and service is illegal, some argue that just looking for signals is no different than listening to broadcast radio. In any event, there has been a decline in the practice due to the possible legal issues and the fact that individuals and institutions are more aware of the need for wireless security. Although corporations are usually targeted, an individual's home-based wireless network may also be noted. By setting usernames and passwords these networks are safe more often than not. Some Web sites, such as www.wifimaps.com, will list wireless hotspots.

BIBLIOGRAPHY

The demise of warchalkers (2003). *Computer Weekly* (June 23). Available at http://www.computerweekly.com/Article122783.htm. Accessed July 21, 2006.

Cybersins and Digital Good Deeds
© 2007 by The Haworth Press, Inc. All rights reserved.
doi:10.1300/5632_20

Watching Over Children
with High-Tech Tools

Can people monitor and protect their children from cradle through college? The answer is increasingly affirmative. Whether this is healthy and beneficial might be another question. Technology affords a number of resources that can be used by parents to keep up with offspring. Some have the potential to save lives as well as grant peace of mind. Included in this arsenal of high-tech tools are devices to watch over infants and young children and technology to monitor teens' activities and driving habits.

In the old days, new parents would often creep into their baby's room just to see if he or she was breathing. Now sophisticated baby monitors and smart rooms can monitor a child's breathing, heart rate, sleeping patterns and positions, and any number of other health-related signals. For toddlers there is the LifeShirt, a spandex garment which children as well as adults can wear at night to similarly monitor their well-being (Alpert, 2005). Once a little one goes off to preschool, mom and dad can check in during the day via webcams. Many summer camps are offering online services with daily e-mail as well as opportunities for adults to watch their kids participate in activities.

The terrible fear of children being lost or abducted can be alleviated a bit by employing tracking devices. Some schools and youth facilities are using carding devices to check children in and out and also monitor their whereabouts on a campus or facility site. Thus a child moving through his or her school day might swipe a card in the library, cafeteria, gym, etc., so that his or her exact whereabouts are known at all times. At a recreation center, parents could keep up with times children signed in and out and keep track of activities in which their children participated. Another way of watching over children is by having them wear garments with electronic tracking devices. One example is SmartWear (www.smartweartechnologies.com), which offers children's apparel such as pajamas, jackets, etc., with RFID. SmartWear also professes to target government agencies, such as firefighters, police, and military, that could benefit from RFID garments (SmartWear, 2006).

Online safety continues to be a concern for parents. In addition to filters and firewalls, other means of verifying that children do not access adult sites are being investigated. One is a biometric device that, when attached to a computer, requires a user's middle finger to be scanned before he or she is admitted to an adult chat room or site. The calcium level of the finger can determine whether the applicant is an adult or child.

As youngsters mature, parental worries are likely to shift to other issues but not necessarily decrease. One special area of concern is the new driver. When preparing a young driver, parents can turn to a number of online and video driving simulators and other training lessons. One well-publicized service for encouraging safe teen driving involves the telephone. Parents put a bumper sticker on the family car which asks HOW AM I DRIVING? and provides an 800 number, thereby allowing themselves to be notified about blatant carelessness and to also remind the teen to drive carefully. OnStar technology can help locate a car in case of an accident. To be even more vigilant, "black box" technology is available. For about $300, a monitor can be installed in a car that reports the location at all times as well as how the car is being handled—whether the driver is making sharp turns, braking suddenly, or speeding.

Should every parent employ every one of the technologies available to monitor every child? Too much supervision might lead to other problems. The term *helicopter parents* has been popularized to describe hovering moms and dads who are overinvolved in children's lives. Even colleges and universities are reporting problems with parents who want to continue very close supervision of their children's studies and activities. When such involvement becomes compulsive, chances arise for problems with the parent-child relationship and mutual happiness and development. On the other hand, potentially lifesaving and beneficial tools can be a boon to both parent and child. As in many things, balance may be the key.

BIBLIOGRAPHY

Alpert, M. (2005). Every Breath You Take. *Scientific American* 292 (February), pp. 94-96

Biometrics Goes One Step Further. (2005). *District Administration* (April), p. 46.

Davis, R. (2005). "Parents Can Act to Keep Teens Safer," *USA Today* (March 2), p. 3B.

Id's to Protect Children. (2005). *Security Magazine 42* (June), p. 24.

SmartWear Technologies: Wearable RFID Solutions. (2006). Available at http://www.smartweartechnologies.com. Accessed July 17, 2006.

Sullivan, L. (2005). Apparel Maker Tags RFID for Kids' Pajamas. *Information Week* 1048 (July 18), p. 26.

Wills, E. (2005). Parent Trap. *Chronicle of Higher Education 51* (July 22), p. A4.

WebXACT

WebXACT is an online service allowing Web site developers to scan their Web pages, one page at a time, to identify accessibility, quality, and privacy issues experienced by users of a Web site. A report is generated for the developers to consider in editing and revising the Web page.

WebXACT is easy to use. Web page developers may go to the WebXACT site (webxact.watchfire.com), enter a URL, and submit their site for analysis. The user then defines how detailed the scan should be by listing what type of items to identify during the scan.

One important scanning measure in WebXACT identifies problems that might be encountered by users with different types of physical disabilities. Among the problems potentially identified include Web page access problems that arise because of hearing or visual impairments.

To accomodate those with hearing difficulties, the developer may wish to consider Web page design alternatives including text references that represent the sounds. Alternatives for those with visual handicaps may include a text-to-speech reading of the material on the screen.

Interface issues, such as access by older browsers and the absence of alternatives to mouse or keyboard, can be identified in WebXACT. In additon, WebXACT can evaluate the accuracy of hyperlinks from the Web page and note any issues tha might emanate from encrypted materials.

Reports generated in WebXACT are broken down by tabs identifying different types of general, quality, accessibility, or privacy issues. There is no charge for scanning a single Web page.

BIBLIOGRAPHY

WebXACT. Available at http://webxact.watchfire.com. Accessed August 1, 2006.

Wiki

Wiki.org describes wiki as "the simplest online database that could possibly work." Another definition continues that wiki is server software that allows users to freely create and edit Web page content using any Web browser. It supports hyperlinks and has a simple text syntax for creating new pages and link between internal pages on the fly. This allows everyday users to create and edit any page in a Web site by nontechnical users.

One of the most popular wikis is Wikipedia. As of July 2006, Wikipedia has more than one million articles covering just about everything imaginable. It is often touted as the great democratizer of information because it allows anyone to write or edit articles. However, by Wikipedias own admission, "unlike other encyclopedias, the volunteer writers of articles in Wikipedia do not need to be experts or scholars. Volunteers do not need to go through any formal process before creating an article or editing an existing article. [Writers] come from countries around the world and are of all ages and backgrounds." Wikipedia's administrators also state that it is policy to add to the encyclopedia only statements that are verifiable, and the Wikipedia style guide encourages editors to cite sources.

In looking at Wikipedia articles of topics that I am familiar, most are pretty accurate. There may be an important source or work that has been omitted, but on the whole the information is correct for the layperson. As with any source, particularly on the Internet, users need to be aware of the authority of the work they are using. Who is the author? What are the sources?

Wiki itself is a great collaboration tool. In this, some distance learning programs are beginning to use online wikis for the development of student course materials, even so far as peer reviewing wikis in juxtaposition of authoritative works. Along these lines, authors and researchers are able to more easily create documents and the like in teams. After all, this is how the Internet was used prior to commercialization.

BIBLIOGRAPHY

Wiki.org. What is Wiki. Available at http://wiki.org. Accessed September 29, 2005.
Wikipedia.org. Wikipedia: Who writes Wikipedia. Available at http://en.wikipedia
 .org. Accessed September 29, 2005.

Wireless Computers and Security

Wireless networking, the ability to connect to a server or network without wire connection, has grown substantially in use during the past few years. The home use of wireless networks or wi-fi has proliferated with the increasing use of inexpensive routers currently selling for under $75. These routers allow any computer with a wireless network adaptor to connect to a home network and to the Internet. Schools have jumped onto the wireless bandwagon as principals and teachers discover the instructional possibilities created by wireless computers with the capability of accessing a school network and the Internet without a copper wire connection.

In homes wireless access to routers allow users within 300 feet or so to connect. Access within a school building is usually provided by more powerful routers that allow network access by students at greater distances.

A degree of security for wireless connections is provided by Wired Equivalent Privacy (WEP), an operating system configuration that allows users to encrypt information exchanged between the individual computers and the router. Schools and businesses with larger security needs are finding that firewalls providing hardware or specialized software security may be necessary.

One additional level of security for wireless users includes the use of virtual private networks (VPNs). VPNs require wireless users to log on to a VPN server with a VPN login. That login affords the wireless user protection from those who could intercept digital exchanges.

The ease of use provided by laptop computers connected wirelessly to the Internet suggests that wireless technology may continue to expand. Such expansion will need to be accompanied by an effort to ensure that wireless users are protected from invasion by those who will try to access their network for fraudulent or destructive reasons.

BIBLIOGRAPHY

Charp, S. (2002). Wireless vs. Hard-Wired Network Use in Education. *T H E Journal* 30(4), p. 12.

McKimmy, P. B. (2003). Wireless Mobile Instructional Labs: Issues and Opportunities. *International Journal of Instructional Media* 30(1), pp. 111-114.

Walery, D. (2004). Wireless Technology in K-12 Education. *T H E Journal* 31(8), p. 48.

"Wireless Warriors; Hobbyists Hunt Networks." (2002). *The Washington Times* (December 9), p. C17.

Worm

The term *worm* refers to an often maliciously created computer program that replicates itself but does not attach to the operation of a program. Instead, the worm is attached to a single file and may be spread from computer to computer when the file is shared.

Often worms are distributed as e-mail attachments. Others automatically send themselves to all e-mail addresses found on an infected computer with instructions to send the worm to all e-mail addresses located on the receiving workstation.

Once the worm is in place, it focuses its impact upon the operating system. The replication causes the computer to slow its processing performance and may, in some cases, cause the computer to fail completely. The impact may soon overwhelm a network.

Even though computer purists refrain from using the word *virus* in reference to worms, vendors who develop virus protection usually include protections against viruses, Trojan horses, and worms. Installing virus protection software is crucial for frequent Internet users.

BIBLIOGRAPHY

Glanz, W. (2000). "Virus Infects E-Mail Networks." *The Washington Times* (May 5), p. 1.

Graham, L. D. (1999). *Legal Battles That Shaped the Computer Industry*. Westport, CT: Quorum Books.

Hunton, J. E. (1998). Facts and Fables about Computer Viruses. *Journal of Accountancy* 185(5), pp. 39-42.

Jacobson, H. and Green, R. (2002). Computer Crimes. *American Criminal Law Review* 39(2), pp. 273-325.

Nicholson, L. J., Shebar, T. F, and Weinberg, M. R. (2000). Computer Crimes. *American Criminal Law Review* 37(2), p. 207.

Index

Page numbers followed by the letter "i" indicate illustrations.

Order a copy of this book with this form or online at:
http://www.haworthpress.com/store/product.asp?sku=5632

CYBERSINS AND DIGITAL GOOD DEEDS
A Book About Technology and Ethics

_____ in hardbound at $39.95 (ISBN-13: 978-0-7890-2953-9 ; ISBN-10: 0-7890-2953-7)

_____ in softbound at $22.95 (ISBN-13: 978-0-7890-2954-6 ; ISBN-10: 0-7890-2954-5)

180 pages plus index • Includes photos

Or order online and use special offer code HEC25 in the shopping cart.

COST OF BOOKS_____

☐ **BILL ME LATER:** (Bill-me option is good on US/Canada/Mexico orders only; not good to jobbers, wholesalers, or subscription agencies.)

☐ Check here if billing address is different from shipping address and attach purchase order and billing address information.

POSTAGE & HANDLING_____
(US: $4.00 for first book & $1.50 for each additional book)
(Outside US: $5.00 for first book & $2.00 for each additional book)

Signature_____

SUBTOTAL_____

☐ **PAYMENT ENCLOSED: $**_____

IN CANADA: ADD 6% GST_____

☐ **PLEASE CHARGE TO MY CREDIT CARD.**

STATE TAX_____
(NJ, NY, OH, MN, CA, IL, IN, PA, & SD residents, add appropriate local sales tax)

☐ Visa ☐ MasterCard ☐ AmEx ☐ Discover
☐ Diner's Club ☐ Eurocard ☐ JCB

Account # _____

FINAL TOTAL_____
(If paying in Canadian funds, convert using the current exchange rate, UNESCO coupons welcome)

Exp. Date_____

Signature_____

Prices in US dollars and subject to change without notice.

NAME_____

INSTITUTION_____

ADDRESS_____

CITY_____

STATE/ZIP_____

COUNTRY_____ COUNTY (NY residents only)_____

TEL_____ FAX_____

E-MAIL_____

May we use your e-mail address for confirmations and other types of information? ☐ Yes ☐ No
We appreciate receiving your e-mail address and fax number. Haworth would like to e-mail or fax special discount offers to you, as a preferred customer. **We will never share, rent, or exchange your e-mail address or fax number.** We regard such actions as an invasion of your privacy.

Order From Your Local Bookstore or Directly From
The Haworth Press, Inc.
10 Alice Street, Binghamton, New York 13904-1580 • USA
TELEPHONE: 1-800-HAWORTH (1-800-429-6784) / Outside US/Canada: (607) 722-5857
FAX: 1-800-895-0582 / Outside US/Canada: (607) 771-0012
E-mail to: orders@haworthpress.com

For orders outside US and Canada, you may wish to order through your local
sales representative, distributor, or bookseller.
For information, see http://haworthpress.com/distributors

(Discounts are available for individual orders in US and Canada only, not booksellers/distributors.)

PLEASE PHOTOCOPY THIS FORM FOR YOUR PERSONAL USE.
http://www.HaworthPress.com   BOF06